STEM Secrets When Success is the Only Option

8 Easy Ways to Make Success Faster, Avoid Burnout and Being Overwhelmed

Jeffrey Harvey P.E.

Apollo Digital Group LLC

© **Copyright 2023 by Jeffrey Harvey - All rights reserved.**
The content contained within this book may not be reproduced, duplicated or transmitted without direct written permission from the author or the publisher.

Under no circumstances will any blame or legal responsibility be held against the publisher, or author, for any damages, reparation, or monetary loss due to the information contained within this book, either directly or indirectly.

Legal Notice:
This book is copyright protected. It is only for personal use. You cannot amend, distribute, sell, use, quote or paraphrase any part, or the content within this book, without the consent of the author or publisher.

Disclaimer Notice:
Please note the information contained within this document is for educational and entertainment purposes only. All effort has been executed to present accurate, up-to-date, reliable, complete information. No warranties of any kind are declared or implied. Readers acknowledge that the author is not engaged in the rendering of legal, financial, medical or professional advice. The content within this book has been derived from various sources. Please consult a licensed professional before attempting any techniques outlined in this book.

By reading this document, the reader agrees that under no circumstances is the author responsible for any losses, direct or indirect, that are incurred as a result of the use of the information contained within this document, including, but not limited to, errors, omissions, or inaccuracies.

ISBN: 979-8-9866340-4-3 (pbk)
ISBN: 979-8-9866340-3-6 (ebook)
Publisher: Apollo Digital Group LLC, Wyoming
Website: www.apollodg.us

Contents

About Author V

Introduction 1

1. Self-Awareness 7
    The Importance of Self-Care
    Beating Burnout

2. Overcoming Frustrations, Expectations, and Failures 31
    Why You Should Not Leave Frustration Unhandled
    Why Failure Is Just as Important as Success

3. Be Fearless and Have the Right Attitude—Learning 47
    Demonstrate Your Capacity for Growth by Tackling Challenges
    How to Make Yourself Invaluable as Quickly as Possible

4. Developing a Growth Mindset   63
   What Is a Fixed Mindset?
   How a Growth Mindset Keeps You Competitive in a Changing Workplace

5. Embracing Emotional Intelligence for Success   81
   Components of Emotional Intelligence
   How to Improve Your Emotional Intelligence

6. Networking   103
   Top Networking Skills That Will Push Your Career Forward

7. Communication   137
   Workplace Communication Explained
   How to Communicate Effectively as a Leader

8. Driving Your Own Success   161

Conclusion   177

References   184

About Author

Jeffrey Harvey's over 25 years as a professional engineer in STEM positions grants him unique expertise to answer questions young STEM professionals face. The STEM field is ever-growing, and the need for professionals has never been higher, so helping a whole new generation succeed has become one of Jeffery's driving forces. As a father to three boys—all with STEM-related fields of study and work—and as a professional himself, he understands the struggles this new wave that young professionals face.

Jeffery currently resides in Oklahoma with his lovely wife, two foreign exchange students, and their Basenji dog. In his downtime, he enjoys being outdoors, writing books, remodeling, reading, traveling, and learning about other cultures. His extensive experience in different leadership positions, including Engineering Director, several positions as an Engineering Manager, Accounting related Supervisor, Project Manager for major and minor projects leading all disciplines, and different individual contributor engineering and STEM roles for two Fortune 500 companies, make him a multi-faceted expert that can help any young person achieve their dreams.

Jeffrey is the owner of Apollo Digital Group LLC and the author of the STEM Secret and STEM Short Series. You can find more information at https://www.apollodg.us or you can email me at jeff.harvey@apollodg.us

- Facebook group: STEM U.S. (https://www.facebook.com/groups/415971137297149)

- Facebook page: Professionals in STEM (https://www.facebook.com/ProfesionalsinSTEM)

- Instagram: STEMSecretSeries (https://ww

w.instagram.com/stemsecretsseries/)

- TikTok: stemsecrets (https://www.tiktok.com/@stemsecrets?lang=en)

Are you looking to take the next step in your leadership journey?

Free Downloads

www.apollodg.us

Introduction

Successful people do what unsuccessful people are not willing to do. Don't wish it were easier; wish you were better. –Jim Rohn

Most people think success is one step away, but you might have to fail and try again before you get your desired results. The education system expects perfection, and while this works in your favor in college, the business world doesn't work like that. Rather than perfecting the same routine, you have to get outside your comfort zone and try new things or learn new skills to stay relevant in a diverse and fast-paced world. Moreover, while determination and drive are noble characteristics to have, it's easy to overwork and burn yourself out, which may give you the opposite result of success. In fact, a ComPsych survey held in 2013 found that 62% of over 5,100 North American workers experienced loss of control, high-stress levels, and extreme fatigue (Valcour, 2016).

When you're overwhelmed or burned out, you're not the best version of yourself. As frustration starts to creep in, you may start despising your job, your colleagues, or your boss. You can easily switch from accepting every duty and deadline thrown your way, however unreasonable, to simply hating every minute you spend at work. However, that can be avoided by knowing just the right balance to maintain between your job and personal life, learning to say no, and knowing that it's not people-pleasing or setting unrealistic goals that will get you the early success you desire in your career.

As someone who holds a bachelor's degree in Mechanical Engineering with a Professional Engineering license and has worked in the STEM workplace, I have worked with many up-and-coming young professionals. I remember this young professional named Adam. He was a hard worker who excelled in every work assignment. However, he was constantly comparing himself to his colleagues. Consequently, he began measuring their success against his but failed to realize that they were building different skill sets. Adam's role was different, and he was targeted to help the company in a different way based on his job description. During our extensive coaching sessions, I often picked up that he misunderstood an engineering job as merely a task or checklist to accomplish before being promoted. While he spent his work hours working on the projects I assigned, during the evening, he would try to teach himself what his peers were learning. Within one year, he felt overwhelmed and exhausted and was becoming burned out from the self-imposed perceptions he had about engineering.

Starting a new job can be nerve-wracking, especially when you're fresh from college. It can be challenging to know where to begin or what steps to take and who to ask when you need help. Sometimes you're tempted to say "yes" when asked if you understand your assignment because you fear being judged or considered incompetent, but in reality, you have no idea what to do. Sometimes you're tempted to bite off more than you can chew so you can impress your leaders and get a promotion. As a result, you may find yourself working longer hours with little to no time for your personal life. If you've been facing these issues, then this book is for you. It can also be helpful if you have been in your role for a year or two and expect a promotion. You feel you have done everything that has been asked of you, and you might have even created a mental checklist of what it takes to be promoted. Because of this, you're demoralized when you see your colleagues with the same years of experience getting promoted, and for some reason, you just can't figure out what you're doing wrong.

What to Expect From This Book

Although this book will help lots of professionals around the world, it targets STEM professionals. College graduates entering their first STEM jobs will benefit a lot from reading this book. They will know what to expect, which questions to ask, and how to embrace and learn from failure. They will also be equipped with how to answer interview questions to get their dream jobs or promotions. Young professionals who are overwhelmed by their jobs as a result of setting unrealistic goals, compare themselves to "more successful" colleagues, and fail to achieve or maintain a healthy balance between their jobs and personal lives will also be equipped with how to set realistic expectations and how to be successful within the first few years of their careers.

While this isn't the case for everyone in STEM, some are introverts who find it hard to function for long hours in social groups or even initiate conversation. However, in STEM, no man is an island, as the community is relatively small, and the ability to create and maintain connections will work in your favor. This book will dedicate chapters to teach you how to network and communicate effectively, why it's beneficial, and how to build effective teams.

Another vital area that this book will cover is how to drive your success. While it's okay to rely on others to push you forward and open the right doors for you, you have a part to play. If you don't work hard towards your goal, no one is going to do it for you. If you're confused or unsure how to drive your own success in STEM, then this book is for you. Other areas that will be discussed in detail include how to be self-aware, how to prevent and cure burnout, having the right attitude to learn, developing a growth mindset, staying professional, and embracing emotional intelligence for success. This book will also give real-life accounts of young STEM professionals I have worked with and mentored, their different situations and approaches, and how they eventually realized success and balance in their careers.

Chapter 1

Self-Awareness

It is better to conquer yourself than to win a thousand battles. –Buddha

Work-related stress can easily affect your whole life. If you think about it, if you have a 40-hour-per-week job, you spend most of your conscious time at work. While work-related stress is sometimes inevitable, the truth is that stress doesn't boost your morale, productivity, or commitment. In fact, the opposite is often true. When you constantly stress about your job, you may not perform to the best of your abilities. You may be stressed if you experience the following symptoms:

- feelings of loneliness, depression, and worthlessness

- having a hard time relaxing

- mood swings, agitation, and frustration

- feeling like you've lost control

- feeling overwhelmed

Sometimes you need to remind yourself that you either run the day or it runs you. It's wise to have a plan to handle stress when you're drowning in deadlines and pressure. As the old saying goes, "Failure to prepare is preparing to fail." Everyone goes through work-related stress at one point, but what if I told you there's a way to prepare for it and reduce its impact? Self-awareness is the ability to focus on the positive when in a negative situation, recognize a bad habit and how it affects your life, and know your emotional triggers so you can rise above them. Do you know your triggers? Do you see your glass as half full rather than half empty, regardless of the situation? Finally, are you aware of your bad habits and how they affect your productivity at work?

The Importance of Self-Care

The demands of life, especially work, can be very hectic to the point that the idea of prioritizing self-care seems far-fetched. However, everything starts with self: If you're unhappy, under unbearable pressure, or intensely stressed out, then performing your day-to-day duties at work can feel like an impossible task. When you choose to do things that enhance your happiness, peace of mind, and well-being, that is self-care. Self-care positions you well to effectively handle stress, relationships, work, and life in general. Most people wait until their stress levels are through the roof before they start taking good care of themselves, but you'll do well to indulge in self-care as a means to combat stress and pressure. A good way to be intentional about prioritizing self-care is to establish your career goals. Where do you see yourself in the next two years? Do you want a promotion, to shift to a different STEM field, or to head an entire department? After establishing your short and long-term career goals, ask yourself if you're on the right path to realizing the goals. If you find that taking on extra work to try and gain recognition at work leaves you burned-out, unable to carry out your main duties, and frustrated, then you might be on the wrong path and going about pursuing the wrong way. This is where self-care comes in.

Professional and Personal Self-Care: How to Connect the Two

Many think of self-care as an indulgence, but it's actually a discipline that affects your productivity, company bottom line, and competitiveness. Professional self-care should become part of your routine because your job constitutes most of your time (this is the case for many). A study found that employees who take more breaks can be more productive compared to those who don't (Ricklick, 2022). So, while it may feel like taking some time to relax and take care of yourself is a waste of time that you would have otherwise channeled toward work tasks, it is actually what helps you meet your deadlines and stay on top of your game.

Some work environments will not give you room for self-care; no matter how determined you are, they will exploit your time and energy with little to no remorse. However, other companies care about their staff's well-being and will invest resources and time to ensure their employees are well taken care of and getting the work-life balance they need. Moreover, remote working is more prominent now, with some companies even allowing flexible working timetables. It's very important to know the company culture before joining so you can adjust your expectations accordingly. It's equally important to choose an organization that's compatible with your goals. Factors to consider when applying include whether or not they value their employees (if they have a voice and if their time is valued and compensated fairly) and how competitive the environment is (growth prospects).

Types of Self-Care to Incorporate at Work

Even at work, you can incorporate different self-care routines to help you enhance your productivity, reduce stress, and feel motivated. There's no one-size-fits-all, and you can figure out routines that work best for you. Below are some of the most vital examples of self-care routines you can add to your work schedule.

Physical Self-Care

These are the physiological activities you engage in as a way to keep your body running efficiently and effectively. They can range from simple things like brushing your teeth, drinking enough water, and combing your hair to exercising and eating healthy meals. Your health is important, and without it, you won't be able to perform your duties well, so it's best to make it a priority. Today's business world is so busy and fast-paced that many employees seldom have time to take breaks. Although taking breaks while you have a pile of work waiting for you seems like a waste of time, downtime is needed to recharge and refresh your mind so you can be more efficient. A study found that one in ten employees do not take their lunch breaks, and 70% said they eat while they work at least once a week. The same study says that Gen Z staff are even more hesitant to take breaks for fear that their employers won't look favorably on them if they do so (Callahan, 2022). However, the fact still remains that taking breaks is vital to the body and mind and shouldn't be viewed as an inconvenience. Here are some of the things you can incorporate into your routine:

- taking walks during your breaks
- going on a stretch break
- taking the stairs instead of the elevator
- walking or biking to work if possible
- making sure your posture is right (ergonomic chairs, posture correctors, balance ball chairs, etc.)
- making sure your laptop/computer light isn't too bright

Going to great lengths to take care of yourself, even if it means packing a healthy lunch or going to the gym before or after work, is a way to ensure you're effective and competent at work (both of which are vital characteristics to get promoted and move forward in your career). It's almost typical for STEM professionals to have hectic work schedules, but you can certainly do seemingly small but significant activities that will keep you healthy, sharp, and productive.

Emotional Self-Care

Emotional self-care goes hand in glove with self-awareness. You need to identify what you're feeling and figure out how to feel it in a way that promotes peace and harmony within you and those around you. The temptation to sweep your feelings under the rug is always there, but suppressing your feelings will only facilitate a later reaction or expression that is otherwise unhealthy and sometimes destructive. For example, rather than doing all the work in a teamwork assignment and not communicating your disapproval to your colleague might eventually lead to losing your temper. Consequently, you might look like the bad guy and lose your good reputation (a good reputation will take you far in STEM). Below are some emotional-care tips you can practice at work:

- Don't be too hard on yourself when you make mistakes. If you're always doing everything right, then perhaps you're not learning new skills.

- Take time to figure out how you feel each day and if you need anything.

- Don't be your worst critic. Your self-talk is very important as your mind always pays attention to what you say. Instead, try to always be your best cheerleader.

- Accept compliments, admiration, and praise from others when you've done well.

- Don't take on more tasks than you can handle to try and impress your boss.

- Run your own race; don't compare yourself to others.

- Celebrate your achievement, even the seemingly small ones.

- Avoid office gossip or conflict; always try to resolve conflict calmly and professionally.

Mental Self-Care

Stress is inevitable; you can experience stress at home, which will affect your performance at work, or get stressed out by your colleagues, tasks, or workplace politics. However, when you engage in mental self-care, you do activities that help you to psychologically cope with stress, anxiety, and even depression. It's important to declutter your mind and keep it sharp so that when you show up at work, you show up in every aspect expected of you. Here's a list of some of the mental self-care tips you can start incorporating into your routine:

- Keep your desk or workspace clean and organized.

- Take your breaks outside your office or away from your desk.

- Rejuvenate your brain by taking 10-minute breaks after every hour or 90 minutes.

- Do some breathing exercises.

- Declutter your brain by creating a to-do list so that instead of memorizing everything you need to do, you'll put it on paper instead.

- Avoid responding to work emails or calls when you're off the clock (set boundaries and stick to them).

- Take time to reflect on everything you're grateful for.

- Avoid putting yourself under pressure by setting realistic work goals and deadlines. Don't promise to hand in something earlier than you actually can.

- Take advantage of support groups or provisions offered at your workplace for mental health.

Social Self-Care

Maslow's hierarchy of needs speaks of love and belonging and our need for friendship to keep us going (Hopper, 2020). From ancient times, people walked and hunted in groups to give them power and leverage over wild animals and sometimes rival groups or tribes. They believed that they were stronger together, and being a loner was probably viewed as a weakness. Workplace teams of today are no different from this concept. You achieve better and faster results when you work as a team and in congruence with each other. Not only is developing strong relations with your colleagues a need, but it's also a strength, and you should make it a priority. When you get along well with your workmates, you feel that you belong, making you feel safe and accepted. Never underestimate the positive effect that can bring to your professional and personal life. Here are some of the things you can do to ensure the social self-care aspect of your life is catered to.

- Bond with your coworkers by participating in team events and outings.

- Accept lunch invites and also return the favor.

- Never miss work volunteer events.

- Make connections with people in the STEM industry, even outside of your workplace.

- If you work remotely, invite coworkers to Zoom meetings so you can get to know each other better.

Spiritual Self-Care

Spiritual self-care means different things to different people. For some, it entails getting and staying connected to a higher power, and for others, it means getting in touch with your values and staying connected to what is happening in the present. Here's what incorporating a spiritual self-care routine can look like:

- Embracing nature and appreciating its beauty (you can work outside for a few hours, take a nature walk during your break, or position your desk to see the sky and trees outside).

- Choose a nice image for your computer screensaver.

- Use the power of your imagination by visualizing yourself relaxing by the beach, taking a hike, or doing your favorite activity. This is especially useful when trying to combat stress.

- Take deep breaths and meditate.

Did Someone Say a Professional Self-Care Plan?

It's important to be intentional about self-care at work, and creating a plan is a good start. When you don't have a plan in place, it's difficult to stay focused on improving anything at all, and self-care isn't an exception. Below is a detailed outline of how to create an outline plan that works for you.

Know Your Stress Levels

Try to pay attention to your stress levels and how your body reacts. If you suddenly experience headaches, lack of morale, low productivity, short temper, and procrastination, then your body might be trying to communicate something to you. Pushing yourself to keep working might not help, but you can refer to the types of self-care discussed above and try to incorporate one or more of them into your routine.

Reflect on Your Stress-Coping Methods

Do you lash out at your coworkers, take various medications to relieve your stress, or drink or smoke when you're stressed out or under pressure? If so, can you honestly say that it has helped you with productivity or morale in the long run, or it's now part of your problems? As Einstein said, "Insanity is doing the same thing over and over again and expecting different results" (Wilczek, 2015). If you've been coping with the work stress and pressure using one or more of the above-mentioned, it's time to revise your methods and choose healthier coping mechanisms like taking time off, setting goals and sticking to them, enjoying physical activity, reading a book, and more. Whatever makes you the happiest, just make sure you deal with stress in healthy ways that will help boost your morale and increase your productivity in the short and long run.

Know Your Triggers

Have you figured out what causes you stress in your workplace? Is it a lack of rewards, little to no recognition, low income, too much work, unrealistic deadlines, office gossip, or abusive bosses? Whatever it is, knowing the root of your stress can help you to either avoid your triggers or face the problem head-on. For example, if you have an unrealistic deadline, you can try to discuss this with your leader and map a way forward.

Stay Prepared

Lastly, always try to prioritize self-care regardless of your circumstances. If you're currently experiencing bliss at work and all is as it should be, that's great, but have you considered how you'll handle pressure and stress when it hits? Exercising, eating right, getting adequate sleep, and other healthy habits should not be contingent on circumstances. Rather, they should be part of your routine. Try to have an accountability partner to make sure you have someone to encourage you when you're not motivated to take care of yourself.

Beating Burnout

While stress is sometimes inevitable for professionals, experiencing it intensely for long periods of time can lead to burnout. In a quest to gain recognition and promotions at work, people sometimes over-stretch themselves, seldom taking breaks or holidays to give their bodies and minds time to heal. Ironically, burnout can lead to quite the opposite of those aspirations, with symptoms such as cynicism, exhaustion, and a lack of interest in one's work. This debilitating state has been linked to poor health by several researchers. Depression, hypertension, insomnia, and substance abuse are some of the health problems linked to burnout.

Consider Julie's case. When she came to work for me, she was a rising star who took on many assignments and knocked them out of the park. She had the right attitude and a growth mindset, always trying to strive above and challenge herself. However, when I had a one-on-one discussion with her during our mid-year, I realized that despite all her success and how excited she was about it, she made personal sacrifices for her job that were above and beyond. They were sacrifices I wouldn't want any employee to make. It was clear to me that she was out of balance and was not self-aware. Because she always assured me during our monthly one-on-one meetings that she had a healthy balance between her work and personal life, I was surprised to learn how overwhelmed and burned out she was. She desired to be the best at her job and become a leader as soon as possible, and as a result, Julie had missed family events and had not taken any vacation time. As if that wasn't enough, she never said no when she was assigned more work or asked to volunteer.

From this conversation, we sat down and divided up some of her work with others and allowed her to lead and delegate some of the work she was previously doing. We reset her expectations around the workplace and developed a sense of trust between us, where she could open up freely with me. Consequently, she achieved the much-needed work-life balance, and after she moved on to another group, we still had regular conversations so I could evaluate if she was keeping it all balanced.

While Julie's intentions were to be the best at her job and to realize success early in her career, she was at risk of burnout. It's easy to be like Julie, then get frustrated when you don't get the success you work so hard for, but are you really going about it the right way?

The Three Components of Burnout

Christina Maslach and several collaborators conducted research that suggested that burnout is a syndrome made out of three components arising in response to work chronic stressors (Ferron, 2018). Here's an in-depth analysis of each symptom:

Exhaustion

This is the main symptom of burnout. People who work for companies that seek their services 24/7 without boundaries are at risk of exhaustion. It can also result from having too many tasks, unreasonable deadlines, or simply not possessing the relevant skills for your job. Because exhaustion causes extreme cognitive, emotional, and physical fatigue, it distorts one's effectiveness and morale in performing their job. When you're exhausted, you'll have a hard time showing up for your job and doing tasks that were previously easy and enjoyable to you. You may even fail to stick to routine and concentrate, and suddenly the idea of you working hard to succeed and move forward in your career becomes hazy.

Cynicism

Cynicism is also known as depersonalization, which is the complete opposite of ambition. Simply put, cynicism causes you to psychologically distance yourself from your work. You start to show up to work and perform tasks just enough to not get let go but without any real enthusiasm for the present or future of your profession. People who have hectic workloads or work in organizations full of conflict and inequality can end up lacking motivation for their jobs. Lack of autonomy (even in decisions that directly affect your work) can also lead to cynicism. Consequently, you feel detached from and even irritated by your coworkers, customers, projects, and everything surrounding your job. If you find yourself persistently experiencing this level of detachment from your job, try to figure out the source of your cynicism so you can make an informed decision concerning which steps to take or how to remedy the situation. There are several internal or external factors that can make one lose interest in their work. However, while cynicism can be inevitable, it should be addressed before it starts affecting your mental and physical well-being.

Inefficacy

Inefficacy often works hand in glove with cynicism and exhaustion because when you lack drive and motivation for your job, you start feeling like you're incompetent, unproductive, and efficient. This symptom may mess with your self-esteem as you start worrying about being unable to perform certain tasks or meet deadlines. However, burnout can also start with inefficacy. This is usually the case when people are not given enough resources and support to perform their jobs (time, autonomy, clear expectations, and information). Also, when you don't have good relations with people whose support you need to succeed or receive feedback or recognition, you may start wondering if you're doing your job well and if you're appreciated at all, which also causes inefficacy.

Burnout Recovery and Prevention

Burnout is usually a result of situational factors, and to recover from it, one often has to change their surroundings. Changing your team, job, or organizational level can go a long way in facilitating your recovery. However, there are less drastic steps you can take that are just as effective because leaving your job is not always the answer. In Julie's case, she was eventually going to be burned out if she had not learned to say no, delegate, and create boundaries. Here are some of the strategies I especially found effective in preventing and recovering from burnout.

Prioritizing Self-Care

Prioritizing self-care is key to replenishing and rejuvenating yourself and a way to give your job and colleagues a shot at the best version of you. You have to be intentional about making this a priority, especially if you have a hectic schedule and work-life balance is just a myth to you. Organizing your time is a good way to find gaps in your schedule to do the things you enjoy. For example, you can account for each hour at work using a spreadsheet and re-organize your time accordingly. In your spreadsheet, you can also record how certain tasks or individuals make you feel, then proceed to limit the time you spend around the people who dampen your mood and pair up the tasks you don't like with an activity you like. This is called temptation bundling.

What Is Temptation Bundling?

Temptation bundling involves pairing an enjoyable activity with a behavior that's not pleasurable to you or one that provides delayed gratification or rewards. In simple terms, it's pairing an activity you want to do with one that you have to do. While burnout damages your willpower and reduces your morale, temptation bundling allows you to perform your tasks while doing something you enjoy. In *Atomic Habits*, James Clear gives the example of an electrical engineering student called Ronan Byrne. Ronan was a fan of watching Netflix and was aware of his need to start exercising more. He put his engineering prowess to use by hacking his stationary bike before connecting it to his television and laptop. Ronan proceeded to program his bike so that a Netflix show would only play if he rode at a certain speed. Failure to do so would result in the show automatically pausing until he picked up his pace again.

While temptation bundling might not be this drastic for you, you can use it as a recovery method. To counter symptoms of burnout like procrastination, loss of morale, and loss of zeal for your job, you can start pairing up your tedious tasks with something you enjoy doing. By doing so, you make your tasks more attractive. Gallup conducted a global poll which found that many people dislike their jobs or their bosses. Of the one billion full-time workers in the world, only 15% are engaged at work, meaning 85% are unhappy or unsatisfied with their jobs (Clifton, 2017). Rather than feeling incompetent and inadequate at work because of burnout, try to use this productivity technique to avoid procrastination while improving both your physical and mental health. For example, you can process your work emails while getting a pedicure or eat at your favorite restaurant while conducting a meeting with a difficult client.

Shifting Your Perspective

Undoubtedly, exercising, eating a balanced diet, enjoying nature, and taking time off can help reduce or prevent burnout, but you'll still wake up to go to the same environment that triggers your burnout. How, then, do you ensure you don't end up drowning in stress when you spend most of your time at work? The solution lies in shifting your perspective and adjusting your expectations. Ask yourself what fixed assumptions and unrealistic expectations you have that you can readjust. For example, if exhaustion is your main challenge, evaluate if you're taking on more work than you can handle, if it's possible to delegate, or if you can change the deadlines.

Moreover, if you're struggling with cynicism, which aspects of your job weigh you down, and can you avoid them while you focus on meeting your goals? Readjusting your expectations and perspective will help you gain control over your work, which will go a long way in beating burnout. In Julie's case, she admitted that she was neglecting self-care and taking on more tasks than she should have, which led her to delegate tasks and take some time off to be with her family or go on vacation. She had been going about gaining recognition the wrong way, and as a result, she risked burnout. After achieving a healthy level of work-life balance, she was happier and more optimistic while maintaining a realistic perspective of how much she could handle and when it was okay to say no.

Avoiding Exposure to Job Stressors

There's no real way to avoid your colleagues because you're bound to work together on one project or the next. However, readjusting your expectations of them and setting some ground rules and boundaries of how much you're willing to take and where you draw the line can go a long way in safeguarding your mental well-being. You may get some resistance from your coworkers and even clients at first, but it's best to make it clear that these changes will facilitate better engagement and productivity from you. *Managing Conflict in the Modern Workplace* recorded that 20% of employers and 26% of employees admitted to conflict being prominent in their organizations. Furthermore, 35% of employees said they experienced interpersonal conflict from ongoing misunderstandings or disputes with coworkers or an isolated occurrence. Of interest to mention is how insults or verbal abuse was surveyed at 28% of perceived workplace behavior following conflicts, with the possibility of physical assaults at 2% and physical threats at 5% (Greedy, 2020).

Building Connections

According to a report published by Enboarder (2022), employees who feel connected have a higher chance of experiencing job satisfaction (96%) as opposed to those who feel disconnected (60%). Further, just 13% of those who are connected anticipate leaving their jobs or current roles within the next year, while there's a 24% anticipation rate of employees who feel disconnected from leaving their current roles. Rich interpersonal interactions are key to alleviating burnout, especially when characterized by cynicism and inefficacy. Practical ways of building connections include seeking out coaches and mentors to point you toward effective ways of identifying and initiating beneficial and meaningful learning experiences and relationships. You can also volunteer to coach and advise others as a way to break from a negative cycle and create a sense of accomplishment and relevance.

Chapter 2

Overcoming Frustrations, Expectations, and Failures

Know your enemy and know yourself and you can fight a hundred battles without disaster.
–Sun Tzu

Realistically speaking, it's not easy to avoid work-induced frustration all year long. From unrealistic deadlines to a proposal you worked so hard on only to be shot down, it's normal to feel angry and frustrated. Other sources of workplace frustration include dealing with an egocentric leader, job insecurity, lack of autonomy, long communication channels, monotony, and office gossip. As if that's not enough, some coworkers can be impossible to collaborate with, which can make your life at work very difficult. However, besides frustrations caused by other people, you can fail at a task by failing to deliver on time or not meeting a customer's requirements.

Moreover, you can make mistakes, and sometimes they're so noticeable that you have to put in some extra work to correct them or redeem your reputation. In fact, a survey involving 2,000 workers reported that one in five made critical errors at work, with 12% of employees admitting to taking risks that cost their organization considerable amounts of money. The same survey also revealed that millions of workers made critical errors at work and got away with them (Young, 2021). In the event that you make an error at work, should you consider yourself incompetent and wallow in self-pity, anger, or frustration? The answer is no. There are healthier ways to cope with failure, and it's best to stay prepared because failure is in our nature as humans. Also, whether or not your frustration stems from internal or external factors when it's unhandled, it can lead to more undesirable consequences.

Why You Should Not Leave Frustration Unhandled

You should always strive to handle your frustrations lest they result in unconscious defense and impaired judgment. Sigmund Freud coined the term psychological displacement to explain a mechanism of unconscious defense in which your brain substitutes a new object or aims for goals that are either unacceptable or dangerous in their original form. This mechanism thrives in the face of aggressive impulses and unconsciously transfers wishes, emotions, and ideas into one's mind. For example, after a bad day at work, you can snap at your children as a defense mechanism. Instead of confronting your emotions, you resort to snapping at your family because they are easier to react to compared to your leader, client, or coworkers. However, this defense mechanism will have you stuck in an unending cycle of frustration and guilt because you'll feel guilty after taking your frustrations out on the wrong people, but you'll still go back to work the following day to face the same triggers or situations that frustrate you, and consequently, you may continue to take out your frustrations on the wrong people and in the wrong way, and repeat.

Moreover, this repeated cycle may ultimately cloud your judgment by clouding your critical thinking skills. When you don't express your feelings, you continue to experience anxiety and stress, which can begin to shape how you perceive your environment. As a result, you may start to resist change, reject ideas, miss deadlines, overreact to your clients and coworkers, and more.

An American neuroscientist, Amy Arnsten, scientifically explained the correlation between stress and impaired judgment. She said that the brain releases high levels of catecholamines when one goes through uncontrollable stress. As a result, the brain is rapidly switched from a thoughtful and reflective state to a rather unconscious and reflective state. While this works in one's favor when they are in danger, it's not the best state to be in when one needs to make properly informed decisions or actions.

How to Deal With Frustration at Work: Five Emotionally Intelligent Habits

My experience in STEM taught me the importance of emotional intelligence, a term created by two psychologist researchers in the 1990s. They defined it as one's ability to recognize, understand, and manage their emotions and those of others.

Daniel Goleman breaks it down into five components (Morgan, 2021). These are self-awareness, self-regulation, intrinsic motivation, empathy, and social skills. This section will share how emotional intelligence can set you up for success in your career and your personal life.

Act With Intention: Know Your Triggers

If you don't learn to manage your emotions, they can easily lead you to self-destruction. Whenever you experience strong emotions of any kind (anger, hatred, frustration, disappointment, etc.), take it as your cue to step back and think things through. That gives you a chance to reevaluate the situation and your feelings and figure out the best course of action to take without ruining relationships and burning bridges. If you want to act with intent in response to anything that frustrates you at work, try to establish your triggers. By doing so, your emotions don't catch you by surprise, and you can respond well in any situation.

David Rock created the SCARF model, which effectively allows you to connect with your emotions (Davey, 2021). David claims that the SCARF model is a way to develop language for unconscious experiences to equip you to catch these experiences when they take place in real-time. According to this model, when frustrated, try to identify which of the following triggered your emotions:

- Status—Is the situation a status threat?
- Certainty—Are you unclear about your future or expectations?
- Autonomy—Do you have the power to make your own decisions?
- Relatedness—Do you have challenges connecting to others as they seem inauthentic or unreal?
- Fairness—Do you feel that you're not being treated fairly compared to your coworkers?

When you figure out the answers to these questions in any situation, you avoid allowing your subconscious mind to react hastily.

Tell Yourself the Right Story to Separate Fact from Fiction

We can easily fabricate stories in our minds and take up central roles in workplace drama even when we shouldn't be involved. If you've ever started an argument with your spouse or partner because of a situation you made up in your head until it appeared real, then this will be easy for you to understand. No one can see the next person's intentions unless they assume them from their behavior. This is because intentions are invisible, making them complex to decipher and understand. However, most of our imagined or invented stories about others are inaccurate. More often than not, people may act with mixed intentions, even without being aware. Sometimes, people's intentions are not related to us, and other times, their good intentions hurt us.

Because of our tendency to exaggerate scenarios in our heads, we follow narratives that validate our imaginations and disregard facts. We also tend to think that everyone is out to get us when, on the contrary, everyone might just be minding their own hectic schedules. According to the confirmation bias theory, we ignore positive emotions while highlighting our negative ones. However, when in the face of workplace conflict or frustration, you can separate fact from fiction by asking yourself these questions:

- What is the story I'm repeating to myself?
- How do I know if it's true?
- Are there other possible alternative theories

or explanations, and what are they?

- What part do I play in this situation?
- How do others perceive it?

These answers will allow you to base your analysis on reality rather than fiction.

Manage Your Expectations

While having expectations isn't a bad thing, you need to ask yourself if they are realistic, beneficial, and quantitative. You also need to ensure that you're not basing your accomplishments on external validations because this can be a recipe for disappointment. You may find yourself frustrated if your expectations aren't met, and the reality is that things sometimes take time.

Sometimes the formula to managing your expectations is being kind to yourself and acknowledging your wins. It's normal to want more (promotions, leadership status, salary raise, etc.), but it's also healthy to take a minute to acknowledge how far you've come, the challenges you overcame, and the goals you've already reached. By doing so, you replace impatience, which more often than not breeds frustration, with gratitude and confidence that if you could achieve your goals then, you can achieve them now. You should also manage your expectations of others because when you hold people to certain standards and they fall short, it's easy to get frustrated. Consequently, even the slightest bit of constructive criticism may feel like an attack on your goals or a rejection from your leaders. Therefore, try to set realistic and quantifiable goals and worry about aspects of your job that are under your control.

Learn to Tackle Those Uncomfortable Conversations

Having uncomfortable conversations is key to intelligent conflict resolution. Rather than whine and sulk over a demanding or micromanaging leader, mean client or problematic coworker, you're better off confronting or addressing the situation by having respectful, private, and mature conversations with the person responsible for your frustration so that you can both try and map a way forward. Undoubtedly, confronting conflict contradicts our fight-or-flight basic instinct, but if you train yourself to have uncomfortable conversations despite how much your body seems to contradict those actions, you'll soon grasp the importance of doing so. Effective communication calls for mutual dialogue. That means that you should allow the next person time to speak so that they feel respected and heard. Before having an uncomfortable conversation to resolve a situation, try to ask yourself the following questions:

- What do I want to get out of the conversation?
- What do I want for others?
- What do I want from my relationship with the next person?
- How should I behave to obtain these results?

It's best to figure out what you want prior to having an uncomfortable conversation. That way, you channel the conversation towards attaining that goal and behave in a matter that deserves such an outcome. Also, asking yourself some relevant questions before you act is a good way to avoid expressing your frustrations in a way that may offend the next person.

Think of Challenges as Opportunities to Learn

You can turn your frustrations into a creative force by searching for new and improved methods to handle challenges. Rather than choosing to create chaos at work or doing the bare minimum in response to frustrating circumstances, you can choose to rise above your situations and emerge stronger. Consider how gold goes through a purifying process before it's ready for the market, and once it endures all those processes, it becomes far more valuable. You, too, can adopt this winner's mindset.

Why Failure Is Just as Important as Success

Many of us view failure as something negative, but in reality, it's just as important as success. According to Elon Musk, "Failure is an option here. If things are not failing, you are not innovating enough" (Winley, 2015). Without experiencing failure, there's no real growth; it simply shows that you're not trying new things. Moreover, if you got everything right on your first attempt, you wouldn't really know the importance of having some of the things you have. Ever heard the phrase, *If you're not failing, you're not trying hard enough*? It's indeed true, especially in STEM, as the business world is competitive, dynamic, and forever evolving, making it crucial to keep acquiring new skills and learning more efficient ways of doing things to avoid being redundant. Rather than feel unworthy next time you fail at something, consider all the fantastic ways failure can shape your career. Here's a look at some of them:

Failure Makes You Strong

Everyone goes through failure at some point, but successful people get to the top by not giving up and trying until they realize their goals. Once you set realistic goals (becoming a leader within the next two years, acquiring a master's degree, enhancing the company's bottom line by 10% within the next year, etc.), don't stop finding ways to reach them regardless of how many times you fail. Some of the biggest names had to battle great rejections and failures before getting to the top. People like Albert Einstein and Steve Jobs, among others, failed many times before reaching the bull's eye, and reading their stories can encourage you when you're tempted to give up.

Failure Gives You Direction

In a weird way, failure gives all of us a sense of direction of where we need to readjust and redirect our steps to achieve our goals. It's normal to second-guess yourself or your decisions, but when you dare to try and fail, you can navigate and gravitate toward your goals with more clarity. You can never really know until you try.

Failure Eradicates Fear

Fear of failure can be the stumbling block between you and your dreams. Because of fear, you can get stuck in a comfort zone and then wonder why you're not moving forward compared to others. However, getting a taste of failure will break that barrier and enable you to take risks. It's in taking risks that most people realize their niches or success.

Failure Teaches You to Value Your Achievements

It's okay to be competitive and always aspire for more. More promotions, more money, more degrees, more recognition, and basically more of everything. But where does that end, and is that a healthy approach to life? It's important to take time to acknowledge and appreciate how far you've come and the effort you put into getting there. Taking breaks between success and pursuing the next goal is equally important because the body and mind deserve to rest. When one fails at something, it reminds them of what they actually got right and the effort it took.

Failure Equals Opportunity

Failure allows you to evaluate your moves and see where you went wrong so that you can make the necessary corrections. It's a chance to show yourself how resilient, unstoppable, and ambitious you are. Many people describe themselves as persistent and resilient during interviews, but the true test of this comes when things don't go their way and they keep hitting a brick wall. Do you have an impossible customer? Did your proposal decline? Did your strategy fail? True resilience is seen in not giving up and changing your actions and direction until you achieve your goals.

Failure Equals Experience

Failure allows you to understand life better and approach things differently for better outcomes in the future. Experience is indeed the best teacher, and whether or not the experience is positive, you learn something that you can use to enhance your life and move your goals forward.

The bottom line is that the road to success is not easy. Therefore, always try to accept your failures gracefully and learn something from them. Don't be afraid to try again, ask for advice from those who have already walked the same path and succeeded, and treat yourself kindly for even daring to try.

Chapter 3

Be Fearless and Have the Right Attitude—Learning

I was never afraid of failure; for I would sooner fail than not be among the greatest. –John Keats

There's no running away from the fact that your career success depends on your willingness to learn. The business world is not static, as more efficient ways, approaches, and strategies are established every day to make businesses more competent and profitable in today's fast-paced world. Those who find themselves embracing comfort zones are at risk of stagnation or redundancy in their careers.

Consider Adam's story. He was a hard worker who succeeded in every work assignment. While our company was large, with many offices across the United States, Adam was mostly involved with doing small projects and working with operations to improve various processes. However, whenever he had one-on-one or year-end reviews, he wanted a checklist of how to get promoted. He considered his success at small projects as a measuring stick and a good reason to get promoted, but in reality, he was always involved with projects that followed the same processes and worked with the same team. Admittedly, the projects were different, but the processes were always the same. This means that he kept getting similar experiences over and over with very little growth.

Adam became frustrated and started comparing himself to his class of new employees who got promotions before he did. In one of our conversations, I told him that it was not surprising that his coworkers got promotions before him. I pointed out how they had been very agile and moved to different parts of the company to try different roles. Adam, on the other hand, had not wanted to relocate and learn other areas, probably out of fear of leaving his comfort zone. As if that wasn't enough, he never agreed to work over the weekend, regardless of how tense his schedule was.

The truth is, no matter how successful you are at your job, if you have the same experience, work with the same team, follow the same processes, and refuse to step outside your comfort zone, then you're likely to progress very slowly in terms of getting promoted. Adam had not experienced new failures or learned new things as he lacked a growth mindset, which didn't work in his favor. He assumed a role that was limited to a specific skill, and he didn't perceive the possible danger associated with that. Leaders with employees that are not agile even for short assignments and are unwilling to flex for some weekend work find it difficult to usher their employees toward growth. While they may be solid employees, their career growth may be limited.

Demonstrate Your Capacity for Growth by Tackling Challenges

As soon as they hire new team members, employees are on the lookout for candidates who showcase a willingness to learn new skills and grow. Employers are interested in candidates who portray a willingness to learn new skills and grow.

However, your willingness to grow shouldn't stop in the interview; you should continue to demonstrate it in the workplace by embracing new or emerging technology and embracing new company strategies. Don't be unresponsive to change because change is constant, and being rigid will never portray you as a competent and highly driven individual, both of which are crucial qualities for growth and recognition. This chapter will tell you why it's important to have the right attitude when it comes to learning new skills. It will also equip you with ways to foster learning, adopt a growth mindset, and unlock intentionality.

Your Career Success Depends on Your Willingness to Learn

You might think that perfecting the same skills is the fastest way to get promoted and gain recognition, but this isn't the case. Leaders everywhere are now more intrigued by one's willingness to learn and adapt to change. It's no wonder that's the case because the business world keeps evolving, and you should evolve with it. Candidates who describe themselves as adaptive fast learners have a higher chance of getting their interviewer's attention compared to their competitors. You stand out even further if you go the extra mile to embrace emerging technology and use tangible examples to demonstrate your desire to keep growing and learning. A 2021 Harris Poll survey found that growth potential or willingness to learn tops 81% of a business's priorities (Express Employment Professionals, 2021).

Why Is It Crucial to Always Demonstrate Your Willingness to Learn?

Besides hiring skilled workers, leaders are interested in hiring candidates who fit into their culture. When you show growth potential, you're grabbing your employer's attention and communicating several vital things. Here's a look at some of them:

Your Skills Are Always Up to Date

The business world is anything but static. Consequently, businesses place lots of importance on their teams because they are a unique source of competitive advantage. Moreover, portraying a willingness to stay in line with industry trends and evolve with the times shows that you're a worthy asset to the team and that you're able to add value to the business's bottom line regardless of current trends or unforeseen changes to the political, social, economic, and technological environment.

You're a Worthy Long-Term Investment

The recruitment process can be tiring and costly, and companies aren't interested in recruiting for the same position over and over again. While it's important to be a current fit, you're invaluable if you prove to be a worthy investment, even in the long run. If you showcase an ability to adapt to emerging changes and constantly upgrade your skills, you'll gain your leader's trust.

You Learn Fast

Demonstrating that you're a fast learner will always work in your favor. Whether you're applying for a job, being interviewed, or gainfully employed, you should always strive to highlight that you're a fast learner and showcase it any chance you get. Research shows that while 34% of companies prioritize candidates with the ability to learn fast, the statistics rise to a whopping 52% when it comes to junior roles (Schooley, 2022).

You Thrive in a Team

Companies put a lot of emphasis on teamwork as a means to gain a sustainable competitive advantage. Who can blame them? People and animals alike work better and faster in a team, and being a loner will not work in your favor. To demonstrate your ability to thrive in a team, make intentional efforts to actively listen to your coworkers and leaders, take constructive feedback well and improve accordingly, and finally, show that you're open to new ideas and suggestions. Going the extra mile for your team when the need arises also proves how dedicated you are. Unlike Adam, who was unwilling to bend a little and work during the weekend when needed, show that you can give yourself fully to your work for your team to succeed. This isn't to say that you should ignore your boundaries and get exploited, but it's common for companies to get extremely busy every now and again, making it vital for their teams to be extra hands-on than they're normally required to be.

How to Demonstrate Your Willingness and Ability to Learn

Undoubtedly, there are many ways to prove to your leaders that you can be a valuable asset to their team by being adaptive to change and willing to learn. Here are some of the most effective ways to achieve this.

Give Examples of How Your Ideas Enhanced the Bottom Line

Ever heard the phrase *numbers don't lie*? Indeed they do not, and leaders are aware of this. Interviewers and leaders alike are interested in how you managed to enhance an organization's bottom line before. With the aid of a quantifiable example, clearly state this when applying for a job, salary increase, or even promotion. Whether you're trying to join a new organization or move to a different position within the same company, always be ready to demonstrate and quantify your noteworthy contributions. This shows that you go out of your way to learn new skills and ideas that can benefit the organization as a whole.

Give Examples of Your Self-Teaching Nature

I can't emphasize this enough—you have to keep learning. From industry-specific newsletters, tutorial videos, and industry blogs, the internet provides so many learning platforms. You'd be surprised how standing out from other candidates or your coworkers by volunteering for a difficult assignment and achieving phenomenal results can take you further in your career. Dare to be different and refrain from doing the bare minimum if you're interested in climbing the ladder.

Tech companies are a perfect example of how the industry is forever changing. You can't afford to relax; otherwise, you'll become redundant. If you want to make a lasting impression, make an effort to stay on top of emerging trends without being asked to do so by your leaders.

Embrace Emerging or Cutting-Edge Technology

Many industries are centered on technology. Consequently, whether or not you're in the tech industry, it's crucial to stay up-to-date with technological trends that are specific to your area of expertise. Learn how emerging technology directly impacts your industry and demonstrate hands-on knowledge by making significant contributions to the business. You can also actively participate in supplemental certifications and courses, especially if you're a tech professional. A report by Cybersecurity Ventures estimated that cybercrime will cost the world about $7 trillion in 2022 alone (Farber, 2022). The same report says that if cybercrime were measured as a country, it would be the third largest economy in the world, after China and the U.S . Clearly, new technology applications are affecting the business world. STEM professionals are required to address this issue on every front. From control systems, devices using computer chips, and communication systems by leaders, businesses, and Homeland Security, it has to be all hands on deck.

In my experience, technology has been becoming obsolete at a rapid pace due to cybercrime.

Ask Questions

This tip is especially handy for interview candidates. An interview is not only a one-way experience, but you're allowed to ask follow-up questions. In fact, it's advisable to do this to show that you're dedicated to learning about the organization and fitting into the company culture and team.

While there are several questions you can ask, like an explanation of the job description, company culture, and more, the most crucial question is how the organization will assist you in terms of advancing your career (continued employee education). When you ask this question, you showcase your dedication to pursuing professional development beyond landing the role.

Emphasize Your Commitment to Growth

Speak about a minor or major bump you maneuvered and overcame or a time you got a relatively quick promotion in a previous organization. These kinds of examples demonstrate your hard work, ability to bend or adopt new tasks, and growth mindset. Whatever the example may be, it's valuable if it shows an interest in learning and participating beyond your job description.

How to Make Yourself Invaluable as Quickly as Possible

Going to college and passing all your modules in record time is one thing, and applying your knowledge to industry-specific trends and excelling in your area of work is another. Don't get me wrong, both can be mutually exclusive, but both take work. Working hard, learning new skills, and developing new techniques don't end the day you graduate. In fact, one can even argue that there's more learning to do on the job as this will take a more hands-on, results-oriented approach. According to the 70/20/10 rule (a popular learning and development model), while 70% of learning is attributed to on-the-job learning, 20% of learning takes place socially through our interactions with friends and colleagues, and only 10% of learning can be attributed to formal training experiences (McGarry, 2019). This goes to show how important it is to keep learning even after you land your dream job; hence, it's crucial to success to consider learning a continuous process. One might wonder how it's possible to learn on the job, and rightfully so, given how it's easy to drown in deadlines, meetings, and the already strenuous demands of your job description. However, you can think of learning on the job, not in the strict sense of going for work seminars, signing up for a weekend of training, and the more traditional ways of acquiring knowledge at work (at least not all the time), and you can seek to learn and develop your skills by following these relatively simple and practical steps.

Shadow the More Experienced Ones

Whether you've been working in your field for a few years or just starting out, shadowing more experienced leaders and colleagues is a good way to avoid making errors or creating unrealistic expectations. Moreover, if you've just joined a start-up company, the chances of a training program being available to you are very slim, making it plausible to seek help, direction, or feedback from a team member, leader, or colleague who has more experience in your field. While showing initiative and the ability to think on the go or be decisive is a good way to showcase your leadership skills, it's okay to seek help or mentorship so that you can develop more confidence to do your due diligence on your job and grasp some otherwise complex processes or concepts sooner than anticipated.

Ask Questions

There's no better way to clear up confusion or role ambiguity than by asking questions. When you ask questions, it shows that you're eager to learn and work as a team toward realizing the same goals, which can really set you apart from some of your coworkers. If you've just joined an organization and aren't sure how or where to apply your skills, don't be afraid to ask. This can also be a great way to build relationships and get comfortable in your role. However, asking isn't just for those who have just joined a new organization. You can also ask questions even after you've been with the company for a long time if new ways of doing things are introduced (technology, policies, personnel, etc.). This will help you to continuously improve as an employee. Remember to value others' time by first checking when they are free to answer questions. You also have to be a good listener and embrace constructive criticism so that you can get the best out of your experience.

Experiment

While some people are visual learners, others learn best when taking action. If you fall under this category, don't be afraid to experiment with new ideas or methods of doing things (as long as it doesn't violate any company policies). When you adopt the trial-and-error method of teaching yourself, you get a better comprehension of your duties and put yourself in a position to break down methods and concepts to others so they can learn too.

Talk

Ever heard of the phrase "A problem shared is a problem halved"? If you're one of those people who get clarity and new ideas from talking things out, then by all means, go for it. When you talk to someone about your challenges, confusion, and new roles, you make room for dialogue, however informal, and you could be surprised by the kind of clarity that dialogue could bring about either from the other person or your own thinking process.

Triumph Under Duress

When you join a start-up, no one really has everything figured out, as everyone is concerned with making quick decisions and taking initiative. Everything is so new, and while the company tries to figure out how to make its internal and external environment sync, profits still have to be made, and customers still need to be roped in and impressed. In this situation, you may go through a trial by fire. This means that you will have to solve problems simultaneously, meet deadlines, and tackle challenges while you stay relevant to the organization and contribute to its bottom line. Although this sounds scary, it can help you build confidence and trust in yourself, both of which are crucial characteristics for success.

Statistics reveal a mismatch between employees' willingness to learn and develop their skills on the job and those who actually manage to do so. While 80% of employees acknowledge that learning a new skill would foster more engagement from them, only 56% actually learn more skills (Markovic, n. d.). This shows that although employees are eager to learn, organizations do not always provide the opportunities to do so. While some companies will provide you with all you need to learn on the job, others will trust that you can figure things out on your own. Whichever the case, make it your priority to keep learning and developing yourself so that you stay up-to-date with current trends and new methods of doing things. Don't be afraid to ask, try new things, make errors, and basically do everything possible to improve yourself. It will all work out in your favor.

Chapter 4

Developing a Growth Mindset

The biggest risk is not taking any risk... In a world that is changing really quickly, the only strategy that is guaranteed to fail is not taking risks.
–Mark Zuckerberg

Most interviewers ask you if you have ever made a mistake or blunder and work and the steps you took to correct it. It's never a good idea to tell them you have never made any blunders because this just goes to show that you have never tried anything new or that you're not flexible or willing to grow. Most people who answer this in a satisfactory manner are able to portray how they were willing to go outside their comfort zones to make things right, even without help from their leaders. That shows a growth mindset. One might wonder exactly what a growth mindset entails in an organizational setup. This chapter will equip you with the in-depth knowledge of having a growth mindset, how to attain it, and the effects it has on your career.

A Stanford professor called Carol Dwerk proposed that a growth mindset is an invaluable skill possessed by people with the belief that their success depends heavily on both effort and time (Hastings, 2021). In other words, people with a growth mindset constantly seek to improve their skills and intelligence through persistence and effort. Instead of being utterly satisfied with the skills and knowledge they possess, these people are not afraid to embrace challenges and persist through them, learn from constructive criticism, and learn from others.

Looking at Dwerk's definition of a growth mindset, one can say that people with growth mindsets don't view themselves as excellent or perfect, but they know that they have a lot to learn and are not afraid to make mistakes. They also focus more on the process of growth than the outcome, and they believe that if they practice and persist enough, they can achieve anything they set their mind to.

What Is a Fixed Mindset?

People with fixed mindsets view their talents, intelligence, and personalities as fixed traits that cannot grow. They believe that there's nothing they can do to improve their innate abilities, which is quite the opposite of having a growth mindset.

In an attempt to shed more light on a growth mindset versus a fixed one, Dwerk went on to describe her middle school classroom. She said that children sat according to their IQs, with the highest performers in better seats than low performers. However, she noticed that high performers were afraid to make mistakes for fear of losing their seats. This is what Dwerk went on to describe as a fixed mindset, which would later prevent "high performers" from tackling challenges or obstacles. These same individuals would also avoid the smallest of obstacles and shy away from trying new ways of doing things because their desire to continue looking smart outweighed their desire to learn. Moreover, Dwerk suggests that 40% of students have a fixed mindset. Consequently, they tend to easily give up, resent the success of their peers, and are constantly under pressure to prove their intelligence (Louick, 2022).

How to Cultivate a Growth Mindset

Cultivating a growth mindset takes effort and consistency. You have to make up your mind to be someone who strives to enhance themselves regardless of how challenging it can feel, especially if you have always had a fixed mindset. Here's a look at effective ways to develop a growth mindset.

Associate With People Who Have a Growth Mindset

Finding solutions to modern-day business problems and being innovative can prove difficult, especially given that systems are always evolving. Besides feeling stuck and not knowing which direction to take or whether or not innovation is the correct move for a particular problem or situation, it's possible to get tired of constantly finding new ways to do things. However, associating with people who have a growth mindset can help you stay motivated because knowing that you're not the only one seeking to constantly evolve and seeing the positive rewards it yields for others is in itself a push factor. According to Marslow's hierarchy of needs, love and belonging also entail belonging to a group and performing as effectively as the next person

(Hopper, 2020). When you pair this up with the fourth need (esteem), you'll realize that one's ability to attain self-respect lies heavily in their confidence to attain growth for self or in a group and to make noteworthy contributions and accomplishments.

Therefore, it's crucial to always seek out people with a passion for experimentation and a commitment to learning, for by doing so, you can attain love and belonging (third on Maslow's hierarchy of needs) with individuals that usher you towards constant growth. Such people are always able to show the resilience necessary to overcome future challenges.

Ask Questions and Take Risks

Regardless of how tempting this is, avoid playing it safe. You can hardly move forward and innovate in this fast-paced world without taking risks, and contrary to popular belief, risk-taking is in itself a strength. However, risk-taking requires a level of acceptance; you should know that success isn't always guaranteed and that failure is not the end of the world. You should treat failure as an opportunity to learn and ask important questions rather than the end of the road. This is where being inquisitive comes in as you ask yourself and others what you might have done better to obtain your desired results before you try again. If at any point you do not remember what a growth mindset is, at least remember that a growth mindset removes the fear of failure.

Establish Where You Stand Now

It's hard to know which direction to go if you don't already know where you are. Similarly, it's important to figure out if you qualify as someone with a growth or fixed mindset, and it's even easier to do so using the fixed mindsets vs. growth mindset table above.

Know Why You're Interested In Developing a Growth Mindset

Again, this is about figuring out your direction. You may find being innovative and trying out new ways of doing things challenging and demotivating at times, but knowing why you do it and what you stand to benefit from a growth mindset will keep you going. This is about figuring out your end game or goal and fixing your mind on it regardless of how tempting it can be to revert to a fixed mindset or a more comfortable zone.

Know Your Limitations

There's a difference between having a growth mindset and setting unrealistic goals. Therefore, it's crucial to be aware of your limitations so that you don't create unrealistic and unreasonable expectations only to get frustrated when you don't yield any results. For example, your genetic makeup can be less suited to certain tasks or endeavors.

Be Mindful of Your Words and Actions

Do you often find yourself saying words like "I'm just not good at this" or "you're just naturally talented?" If so, try to change them to "I'm not good at this yet" or "you must have put in lots of effort to achieve this." Noticing how others speak can help you single out those with growth mindsets so that you can associate more with them.

Don't Seek Approval

Seeking approval can be mistaken for wanting to belong, which is a basic human need, but it can actually limit you. When you seek approval, you focus more on being right rather than innovating and trying out new things, even at the risk of failure. Stretching comes with failure sometimes, but that only means you're embracing a growth mindset rather than staying static.

Rather Than Focusing on Rewarding Traits, Focus More on Actions

I find this to be especially helpful to parents, and it goes hand in glove with operant conditioning. Operant conditioning was first described by B.F. Skinner, a behaviorist who believed in observing the external and observable causes of human behavior rather than motivations and internal thoughts. This theory's premise is simple: Actions that are reinforced are strengthened and highly likely to occur again as a result. The opposite is true; actions that are followed by undesirable consequences are weakened and less likely to occur again (Cherry, 2022).

Similarly, you reinforce your child's behavior more when you focus on their actions rather than their results. For example, instead of saying, "you're very smart," after your child brings back all As, you reinforce positive behavior when you say, "you must have worked really hard for this." This is no different for adults, and it sums up what a growth mindset is: Instead of attributing your success or those of others to their traits, attribute them to actions. Seeking out those actions and understanding them so that you can develop them even further will also work in your favor.

Realities of a Growth Mindset

When it comes to stretching yourself and going for your dreams, it's always good to be realistic. Here's a look at some of the realities associated with having a growth mindset.

It's Possible to Be Somewhere in the Middle

Did you know that it's possible to be somewhere in the middle of a growth and a fixed mindset? Upon analyzing students' mindsets, Professor Carol Dwerk failed to identify utterly binary results. While most students leaned more toward one side or the other, most mindsets were in the middle (Wooll, 2021). For example, those who might have attributed their math abilities to their commitment, attentiveness, and commitment to learning might also have believed that their ability to read and write was inherent. This observation holds water even in the workplace.

Having a Growth Mindset Goes Beyond Effort

Many people believe that having a growth mindset boils down to effort. In fact, Professor Carol Dwerk noticed that teachers held the belief that they could improve a student's performance by telling them to put in more effort. Undoubtedly, effort is crucial, but so is one's overall attitude toward learning and how one views failure.

Not Everyone Has the Ability to Achieve Everything

No one is superhuman; everyone has limitations, even the most seemingly all-around capable people. While having a growth mindset might help combat your limitations, it does not erase them. For example, a male or female who is 5'2 is unlikely to become a runway model regardless of how driven they are. While they might have a growth mindset, society's unjust expectations may limit them.

Positive Outcomes Result From a Growth Mindset and Working Towards a Goal

If you embrace a growth mindset, you know that positive improvement can be achieved. In order to reach your full potential, this knowledge should be accompanied by the following:

- putting in the time
- acknowledging failure as part of the learning process

- embracing challenges

- actively developing new strategies to overcome these challenges

When you chase a goal without acknowledging these facts, you're unlikely to yield your desired results.

The Science Behind a Growth Mindset

Did you know that the notion of a growth mindset can be backed by science? This is because it's closely linked to neuroplasticity, which describes the brain's tendency or ability to continuously change in adults throughout their lives. Neuroplasticity is such a sophisticated and fascinating phenomenon because the connections between one's neurons can change with experience. This means that one has the ability to accelerate or delay their neural growth depending on their lifestyle modulators or behavior. Lifestyle modulators that can accelerate neural growth include good sleep patterns, a healthy diet, and regular exercise. Let's take a look at the two types of brain plasticity.

Functional Neuroplasticity

This can be described as your brain's ability to shift or transfer function from damaged to undamaged regions.

Structural Neuroplasticity

This is the one that's closely linked to a growth mindset. It can be defined as the brain's ability to change its neural connections/physical structure as a direct result of learning.

The theory of brain plasticity stems back from the 19th century, but scientists only started paying attention to it in the 20th century. Psychologist William James claimed that nervous tissues were endowed with fascinating degrees of plasticity (Berlucchi & Buchtel, 2008), but researchers concluded that changes in the brain were only possible during childhood or infancy. However, by the 1960s, James's hypothesis came to light again as a growing body of supporting evidence found that healthy parts of the brain could partially take over functions destroyed by a stroke.

Further research revealed that while brain plasticity declines with age, it doesn't come to a standstill as new neurons can keep appearing in certain parts of the brain until one's last moments. Of interest to mention is the most popular example of neuroplasticity involving London bus and taxi drivers. While taxi drivers were discovered to have a larger hippocampus, bus drivers were found to have a relatively smaller one (Maguire, Woollett, & Spiers, 2006). The hippocampus is the structure of the brain that plays a significant role in memory and learning.

While the reason behind this is fascinating, it's pretty straightforward. Bus drivers followed strict and pre-planned routes, but taxi drivers had to memorize and remember different backstreets, corners, and detours as they navigated across the city. This means that they regularly stimulated their hippocampus, and by doing so, they changed their brain structure.

This example reminds me of Adam and his unwillingness to work in different parts of the company or take up different roles. Regardless of how I would go out of my way to give him different assignments to help him grow, he was basically only sharpening his skills without learning new areas or challenges. Just like London bus drivers, if you follow the same routine without challenging yourself to think outside the box, your growth will be limited. However, when you expand your area (gaining new skills and insights), you will not only learn how to solve problems, but you will grow at a remarkable pace.

Five Practical Examples of a Growth Mindset

Now that you know what a growth mindset is, it's time to look at some of the most practical ways you can apply it at work. This may take practice, but so does everything else in life. Oftentimes, people believe they have a growth mindset, but they don't realize that sometimes it's easier said than done. Let's say you go for an interview, wow the interviewers with your enthusiasm to learn, and grow an unmistakable passion and zeal for the role. You get the position, kudos to you, but how are you going to display the growth mindset you so openly portrayed during the interview in real time? My point is it's one thing to say you have it, and it's another to practice it. I would even go a step further and say that it's possible to maintain a growth mindset in some scenarios and a fixed one in other situations. Here are some of the ways to apply a growth mindset in the workplace (Jongen, 2022):

Don't Take Feedback or Criticism Personally

Unless your leader is out to get you (which is hardly ever the case), their criticism or feedback should never be taken personally. A growth mindset seeks to listen, learn, and improve. No matter how good you are at your job, you won't always get things right, and even if you do, sometimes there's room for improvement. Technology is always advancing, and businesses are constantly finding new ways to do things. If you find yourself on the receiving end of negative feedback, take it as an opportunity to learn, ask questions, and improve your skills accordingly.

Don't Be Afraid to Accomplish New Tasks

Feeling a little bit nervous when you have to accomplish new tasks is normal, but don't allow that anxiety to cripple you. The more you get outside your comfort zone or routine to try new things, the less nervous you will be about failure. A fixed mindset will think, "This is not my area of expertise," or "I will never get this right." On the other hand, having a growth mindset will make you certain that although you're outside your usual routine, you will learn until you get things right. Remember to take failure as an opportunity to know which areas need improvement.

Go for Task or Job Rotation if You're a Leader

It's important for employees to keep developing new skill sets, and leaders are in a good position to promote this. A good way to do so is by choosing tasks or job rotation over fixed roles. This way, employees will learn different skill sets, which benefits them. It is also beneficial to the organization because should a certain employee fall ill or be absent for one reason or another, their duties will be easily carried out until they report back for duty.

When You Hire New Staff, Pay Attention to Whether or Not They Are Willing to Learn New Skills

Make it a priority to hire staff who are willing to learn new skills, among other things. It's easier to implement tasks or job rotation with people who are not only willing to do it but are enthusiastic about it. It's okay to hope that people with fixed skills will catch up with others and be willing to learn, but if that isn't the case, they may negatively influence their teams or demotivate those willing to grow.

Think of New Strategies, Tasks, and Actions as a Process and Not an Event

When new processes of doing things are introduced, it's better to think of the change that comes with them as a process and not an event. Also, rather than seeking success, seek to gain new insights and learn new things. You're in a much better position to succeed when you concentrate on learning rather than on the end result.

How a Growth Mindset Keeps You Competitive in a Changing Workplace

Now more than ever, jobs require us to keep evolving. Of interest to mention is the report by McKinsey that states that about 375 million workers worldwide will need to learn new skills or change their roles by 2030 (MacKay, 2018). This might be a scary thought, but those with a growth mindset are in a better position to move with the times and remain relevant in a competitive and dynamic business world.

RescueTime gives a hypothetical scenario where you're running a small agency with two different developers (MacKay, 2018). One had a fixed mindset, and the other a growth one. Consequently, the fixed mindset developer is focused on handling business as usual. This means they are more inclined towards using languages and techniques that have worked in the past. They are also reluctant to try new things as they solely rely on their talent.

On the other hand, the growth mindset developer believes in constantly trying new solutions. As a result, they are more inclined towards seeking new opportunities to try out or test new and future-based coding languages. They are aware that they may fail at first, but they take it as a learning opportunity to become a better coder. Looking at these two examples, who would you want on your team?

With a growth mindset, you will go beyond thriving in the face of challenges. You will exercise the freedom to push your limits and reach for the sky. As if that's not enough, you will not hesitate to be creative and challenge yourself every single day. If that won't push you forward in life, what will?

Chapter 5

Embracing Emotional Intelligence for Success

We are dangerous when we are not conscious of our responsibility for how we behave, think, and feel. –Marshall B. Rosenberg

Emotional intelligence can be described as the ability to be aware of, control, and express your emotions, as well as handle interpersonal relationships empathetically and with good judgment. Moreover, emotional intelligence is crucial because it unlocks both professional and personal success. It not only has the power to influence how you perform at work, but it can help you gain success without burning yourself out. This chapter aims to help you understand emotional intelligence in the workplace. In this context, you can think of emotional intelligence as the capacity to recognize and understand your emotions and skills in a way that allows you to manage your relationship with yourself and with others. Needless to say, it's crucial for you to maintain healthy relations with your workmates (subordinates, leaders, and colleagues) and to build and maintain beneficial relationships with customers. No man is an island, and teamwork is at the heart of many organizations.

Consequently, you'll be expected to interact with others, which calls for mutual respect even when opinions differ. One may even argue that academic qualifications alone are insufficient when it comes to realizing success in the workplace and that emotional intelligence may hold more weight and push you forward faster than your qualifications. If you have ever been around highly educated people who lack emotional intelligence and are unable to accept other people's opinions, then you know what this looks like, and chances are these people climbed the ladder a little slower than their counterparts, if at all.

Components of Emotional Intelligence

There are five components of emotional intelligence, according to Daniel Goldman, who holds a PhD in psychology from Harvard and is a co-founder of the Collaborative for Academic, Social, and Emotional Learning at Yale's Child Center Studies (Craig, 2019). Goldman identified emotions on a non-verbal level and outlined how to use emotions as a guide for cognitive thinking. He also aimed to help one understand the information conveyed by their emotions, the actions they can provoke or generate, and finally, how one can regulate their own emotions. The components of emotional intelligence are as follows (Cherry, 2018):

Self-Awareness

As discussed in Chapter 1, self-awareness is the ability to recognize and understand emotions (yours and those of others) and to be aware of how actions, emotions, and moods take effect. It also involves monitoring one's emotions and taking note of the reactions that accompany them. When you're self-aware, you know that there's a relationship between your feelings and actions, and you seek to use your strengths and limitations to get the most out of this relationship.

Most interviewers ask what your weaknesses are and what you can do to improve, and candidates who stand out are able to showcase their awareness of areas that need improving and a plan of action to do so. In Adam's case, it was crucial for him to realize that his fixed mindset slowed him down in terms of getting the promotion that he so desired and that he needed to get outside his comfort zone and learn new skills or go the extra mile for the benefit of his team. This is a good example, but every person has weaknesses and strengths, and knowing what to improve or capitalize on is critical.

Self-Regulation

Self-regulation is a vital part of emotional intelligence and will help you stand out in the face of internal and external organizational changes. It not only entails the appropriate expression of one's emotions but it's characterized by the ability to be flexible. You will thrive in managing and resolving conflict as well as diffusing tense situations that would otherwise cause divisions and chaos in work teams. Self-regulation also entails being aware of your actions (how they affect others), taking responsibility for otherwise controversial actions, and mending relations.

Social Skills

Social skills, in this case, involve the ability to interact well with other people (colleagues, leaders, etc.). It's important to understand one's emotions in order to cultivate beneficial interaction or effective communication with others. There are various forms of social skills, including active listening, verbal and non-verbal communication skills, developing rapport, and leadership. When Julie opened up to me about the many sacrifices she had been making for her job, I gave her constructive criticism, which she reciprocated by actively listening to me before implementing change. Social skills come with such benefits, and you'll achieve so much more when your interactions with others are positive.

Empathy

Empathy is your ability to understand other people's feelings, allowing you to respond appropriately to them. Empathy is at the center of mutually respectful human interactions, and it plays a vital role in maintaining good relations in the workplace. Empathetic people are able to understand power dynamics and their impact on feelings and behavior.

Motivation

Motivation, in this case, is viewed in light of intrinsic motivation. This entails being driven by the need to meet personal goals rather than being driven by external factors like fame, recognition, and money. In most cases, people who are intrinsically motivated find drive and fuel their fire by immersing themselves in activities they find motivating and stimulating. Such people are not only action-oriented but also set goals and always look for ways to improve themselves. They also stand out and are easily noticed in the workplace because they are committed to their work and take initiative.

The Influence of Emotional Intelligence on Job Performance and Burnout

To understand the impact of emotional intelligence on burnout and job performance, one has to understand what psychological capital is. Psychological capital can be defined as one's positive psychological state of development, characterized by having significant levels of hope, self-efficacy, resilience, and optimism. As we progress, you'll learn that emotional intelligence has a positive impact on one's psychological capital and how this all aids in enhancing job performance while reducing burnout.

In a quest to answer the following questions, a survey involving 450 employees from various enterprises was held through questionnaires (Gong, Chen, & Wang, 2019):

- How does emotional intelligence impact job burnout and job performance?

- Is the impact direct or indirect?

- What role is played by psychological capital?

The following conclusions were reached:

- While employees' emotional intelligence is negatively correlated with job burnout, it was found to have a positive predictive effect on both job performance and psychological capital.

- While psychological capital has a negative predictive effect on job burnout, it has a positive predictive effect on job performance.

- Psychological capital has a mediating role when it comes to the relationship between emotional intelligence and job performance/burnout.

Overall, when you improve your emotional intelligence, your psychological capital is enhanced. High psychological capital leads to better job performance and reduced job burnout.

Significance of Emotional Intelligence in the Workplace

The business world is fast-paced, and it continues to develop rapidly. One of the key indicators of a growing enterprise is organizational performance; when it's inadequate, the business is at the mercy of competitors. According to Porter, five forces shape every enterprise and help them separate their strengths from weaknesses (Wright, 2021). These are:

- competition in the industry
- threat of new entries
- power of suppliers

- power of customers
- threat of substitute products

The first on the list of Porter's five is competition in the industry. The larger the number of competitors and equivalent services or products they offer, the higher the competition or the lesser the power a company holds. However, one of the unique competitive advantages an organization holds is its employees, and it really is as strong as its weakest link. If employees are burned-out, demoralized, and unmotivated, an enterprise is weakened and not in a good position to compete against rivals or excel in a fast-paced environment. Undoubtedly, it's crucial for the employees of a company to be motivated and to perform well, and this is where emotional intelligence comes in.

In contemporary society, competition is inevitable, and so is an organization's quest to improve its productivity in order to measure up. However, this translates to increased workload and pressure for employees. Ultimately, this leads to job burnout, and if it's not resolved, it starts a vicious cycle that can only create problems for the organization. Yes, companies seek to hire employees who are willing to surpass their established roles and go above and beyond for the company, but at what cost for both players? Once an employee is burned-out, their performance declines, and with the lack of self-efficacy, they suffer even more severe burnout. In the end, this will negatively affect the organization's productivity as a whole. Moreover, recent findings outline that job burnout has many negative effects on employees, such as reducing job performance and satisfaction and increasing absenteeism and turnover (Maslach & Leiter, 2016). It's clear that reducing employee burnout is key to improving productivity and the performance of the organization as a whole.

It has become apparent that academic qualifications alone will not make you stand out as an employee. Rather, emotional intelligence, which goes hand in glove with psychological capital, will give you the resilience, innovation, and adaptability you need to thrive as an individual, as part of a team, and as a unique competitive advantage to your organization. Here's a look at more reasons why emotional intelligence is important in the workplace:

- It allows you to work towards your goals in spite of obstacles and challenges.

- You can understand your emotions and those of others (harmonious teamwork).

- It fosters healthy communication, which allows you and your team to effectively work towards common goals.

- It creates a deeper connection between teams.

- It gives you the flexibility you need to adapt to change.

- You can make decisions that are best for everyone because you can understand them empathetically.

- You can excel in leadership roles.

Job Satisfaction

While there are various factors that contribute towards job satisfaction (work environment, remuneration, growth opportunities, and recognition), emotional intelligence contributes towards intrinsic factors like emotional well-being, high levels of self-esteem and efficacy, and an overall positive outlook, which all facilitate a sense of being happy and satisfied in one's role. Consequently, one also experiences significantly lower levels of stress and burnout, both of which can cause one to lose passion and zeal for their job. Moreover, when you're satisfied with your job, your productivity, engagement, and loyalty increase while your levels of absenteeism and chances of turnover decrease.

Job Performance

Job performance goes beyond meeting deadlines and showing up to work every day. It goes beyond a dedication to driving results and meeting the company's bottom line because if you're unable to be consistent with your approaches, you'll go back to the drawing board and start all over again. If Julie, regardless of how hardworking, determined, and resilient she was, had continued on the path of neglecting her personal needs while she went above and beyond for her job, she would have eventually been burned out. There's a strategy to exert yourself fully to your job that allows you to be consistent, and that's where emotional intelligence comes in. In fact, according to research about studying skills critical in the workplace by Bradberry (n.d.), emotional intelligence was found to be the most effective or strongest predictor of job performance, accounting for 58% of success across forms of jobs. The same study also found that 90% of top performers scored high for emotional intelligence (EI).

Moreover, the Institute of Health and Human Performance conducted research that came out with the following results (Bradberry, n.d.):

- Over 80% of competencies differentiating top performers belong in the EI (emotional intelligence) domain.

- Organizations with executives who have high levels of EI have significantly higher chances of being profitable.

- Upon implementing stress management and EI training, a Motorola manufacturing site enhanced employee productivity by 93%.

Industrial Relations

Emotional intelligence helps build and maintain harmonious industrial relations. It gives you the ability to comprehend non-verbal cues, and as a result, you can avoid conflict before it blows up or fix a situation before it becomes a problem. For example, you can notice a coworker exhibiting some non-verbal cues of frustration and show them empathy or resolve the issue before it's too late. Furthermore, when you have high levels of EI, you're self-aware, which allows you to identify any problematic behaviors you might be exhibiting and fix them before they create problems between you and your coworkers, leaders, or even customers. Anyone can have a bad day at work, and even the most satisfied and motivated employees can appear grumpy or uncooperative as a result. However, self-awareness will help you avoid your triggers or focus on more positive thoughts when you're not having the best day. This is important because, regardless of your situation, business, more often than not, has to go on.

Self-Development

Self-development is often considered as acquiring more skills and competencies, but your behavior in the workplace can set you up for success. This is because leadership skills and emotional intelligence go hand in hand as they are both characterized by abilities such as patience, empathy, active listening, self-awareness, decision-making, and positivity. Such abilities will help you to advance early in your career by either being promoted to leadership roles, being promoted, or getting a raise.

Motivation

You can encourage your coworkers to have strong interpersonal skills by leading by example. When everyone in your team develops empathy and responsibility, you're much more effective and able to achieve your short and long-term goals with much more ease. Being a positive role model to your coworkers will also set you up for a promotion to leadership roles, perhaps faster than your qualifications.

How to Improve Your Emotional Intelligence

Yes, you can develop and enhance your emotional intelligence. However, just like learning, it's an ongoing process with a journey that differs for each individual. Margaret Andrews lists the following steps as a means to develop emotional intelligence and enhance intrinsic abilities like empathy, self-awareness, and social skills (Harvard Professional Development, 2019).

Know Your Emotions by Name

It's important to know your emotions and be able to name them, especially when you're in a stressful situation. Try to identify what emotions typically arise when you're stressed or under pressure and figure out how you would prefer to react in those situations. Are you able to pause for a moment and reconsider your response? When you're able to pause and name your emotions and alter your response or reactivity accordingly, you're one step closer to developing your emotional intelligence.

Ask For Feedback

It's not always easy to ask other people's opinions of you and how you react to different situations, but it's beneficial. Therefore, you can ask your leaders, colleagues, friends, and family to rate your emotional intelligence on a scale of one to ten. Examples of questions you can ask them are how you normally respond to stressful or difficult situations, how well they'd say you handle conflict, and how empathetic and adaptable you are to various situations. Be ready to take constructive feedback without being defensive and seek to improve where you recognize weakness.

Read

Several studies reveal that reading literature enhances emotional intelligence (Jones, 2018). Not only does reading improve cognitive function, but it facilitates what scientists call refined theory of mind, which refers to how we perceive other people's mental states and how that state helps us predict other people's actions. Moreover, reading stories from different perspectives will not only improve your empathy, but it will help you deeply understand their motivation, actions, and thoughts in a way that helps your social awareness.

Question Your Opinions

Don't risk the danger of thinking your opinions are always right. It's easy to fall into the "I'm always right" trap because the world is hyper-connected, and your opinions can be constantly reinforced by those who share them. In order to enhance your emotional intelligence, it's best to take time to understand the other side of the story and allow your opinions or views to be challenged. This applies even when you deeply believe your views are right. This way, you will not only learn by gaining new ideas, but you will understand other people's thought patterns.

Recognize the Emotions of Others

Emotional intelligence should put you in a good position to build and maintain healthy relationships with others. This will come in handy in the workplace as being able to work well within a team is a positive attribute that will get you noticed faster than your qualifications. Because emotional intelligence entails actively listening to others, you'll be able to empathize with them and work in congruence with them while making your feelings known without offending anyone. Besides work relationships, this will work well for your personal relationships with family and friends.

Emotional Intelligence and Leadership

In order to coach teams, give feedback, manage stress, and collaborate with others successfully, you need high levels of emotional intelligence. Indeed, your technical skills might have helped you secure a job, but will they guarantee a promotion? A person who possesses exceptional technical skills knows how to solve problems, and, overall, a deep thinker might falter when it comes to controlling their reactions in the heat of the moment, making connections with clients or colleagues, or helping people understand things from their perspective. Eventually, their lack of emotional intelligence will hinder their progress as well as the progress of those around them. Can such a person be considered for leadership roles? If they were, would they produce results and keep the company's productivity levels competent enough for this fast-paced world? Let's take a look at these insightful statistics (May, 2022):

The Influence of Emotional Intelligence on Career Advancement:

- Out of 34 essential workplace skills, emotional intelligence was discovered to be the most effective or strongest predictor of performance.

- Highly emotionally intelligent individuals make $29,000 more annually.

- There will be a 26% growth in the demand for emotional skills by 2030.

- 75% of managers evaluate an employee's readiness or eligibility for a raise or promotion using emotional intelligence.

Leadership with Emotional Intelligence

The importance of emotional intelligence for leaders has been a topic of discussion for years, but the COVID-19 pandemic and the subsequent shift to remote and hybrid work made this more apparent. Let's take a look at some of the findings:

- A study found that out of 155,000 leaders, only 22% had high levels of emotional intelligence.

- Employees with emotionally intelligent leaders are four times less likely to leave their jobs.

- Managers who address personal issues, lead change, spot talent, and give feedback have high levels of emotional intelligence.

How Emotional Intelligence Benefits the Organization as a Whole

Harvard Business Review and The Four Seasons revealed the advantages of an emotionally intelligent team as follows:

- Less than 20% of companies can be classified as emotionally intelligent.

- Emotionally intelligent companies have relatively better customer service/experience, advocacy, and loyalty.

- Organizations that are emotionally intelligent are more productive, more empowered, more engaged, and more risk-tolerant.

Why Emotional Intelligence Is a Must-Have for Leaders

Leaders are responsible for an organization's outcome, and in a way, they set the tone for the entire organization. Their emotional intelligence, or lack thereof, has far-reaching consequences as they either keep the company competitive and profitable or demoralize employees. When they lack emotional intelligence, an organization can expect to experience high turnover, low productivity, and low employee engagement. As a leader or employee interested in a leadership position, you might do extremely well when it comes to the technical side of your job, but if you can't collaborate well in a team or communicate effectively, then you might not be considered for a leadership role or a further promotion.

Chapter 6

Networking

All successful networking is dependent on two key things: reciprocity and curiosity. –Phyllis Weiss Hasero

Networking is indeed a skill, and it's much easier said than done. However, in any professional's life, its importance can never be underestimated because it opens many doors, even on a social and personal level. You might find it hard to make professional connections or advance your career if you don't possess the right networking skills. If you're wondering what these skills are and how to apply them, then this chapter is for you.

Top Networking Skills That Will Push Your Career Forward

Networking can be defined as interacting with people, particularly those with similar professional goals, in order to build long-lasting and mutually beneficial ties. I think it's important to develop the right networking skills so that your networking efforts are not in vain. Here's a look at some must-have top networking skills.

Interpersonal Skills

Having interpersonal skills allows you to read the room in a social setting and gives you the ability to understand those around you. Poor interpersonal skills mean you lack awareness of others and, as a result, you can't comprehend their emotions, concerns, or needs. Every good leader should be able to pick up on cues and understand why employees behave as they do to motivate them accordingly.

Communication Skills

This is arguably the most crucial networking skill. Communication goes beyond saying something and hearing what other people say. It also goes beyond humor, intelligence, and insight. Effective communication involves being mindful of how you convey your message and receiving other people's opinions without demeaning them. In addition, when you communicate well, you are mindful of your tone of voice, language, and even the posture you assume. All these elements will make or break your networking, depending on whether or not you choose to observe them.

Active Listening

Active listening has less to do with just hearing what someone is saying and more to do with paying close attention to the message they're conveying and asking follow-up questions to ensure you understand the essence of the conversation. Active listening is an important skill that tells the next person that you take them and the conversation seriously. If you constantly check your phone and nod your head absent-mindedly during an interview or meeting, then you're less likely to get the job or be considered for a promotion because leaders will not take you seriously. This is where the golden rule applies: Do unto others as you would want them to do for you. If you want leaders or coworkers to take you seriously, then you should also take them seriously, and what better way to do it than by being an active listener?

Non-Verbal Communication

Non-verbal communication takes up 93% of any verbal message (Scott, 2022). It includes every message you convey without words and can be defined as the use of non-verbal platforms (body language, eye contact, gestures, facial expressions, and posture) to transmit signals or messages. Non-verbal communication is a crucial element of networking as it sets the tone for conversations. If you keep your shoulders hunched and your eyes locked on your phone screen at a work event, you're less likely to be approached by someone who wants to strike up a conversation. The opposite is true for those who radiate positivity and confidence, as they're likely to network successfully and move their careers forward in the process.

Respect

Respect is a must-have networking skill as it makes you approachable and easy to interact with. This may entail active listening, polite body language or facial expressions, and minding your tone of voice. Imagine frowning at a work event because you don't like the food or constantly interrupting people when they speak and never giving them a chance to finish their sentences. If you're cringing at the thought of this, that's how bad it looks to the people around you, and it might drive them away before they get to know you. Being respectful also means controlling your temper, thinking before you speak, and being polite even to individuals who do not hold important positions.

Humor

Research has found that humor is the key to success in the workplace (Smith, 2013). This is because humor draws people closer, allows them to enjoy their interactions, and helps them build trust. Remember to always share positive jokes that are not offensive to anyone. By putting a smile on people's faces, you draw them closer to you.

Confidence

People pay attention to confident individuals. If there's one thing motivational speakers are good at, it's portraying confidence in whatever they say. They are so confident that they may even convince you to start a chicken business with one chicken feather. Interviewers also look for confidence when they hire for sales and marketing positions because people are likely to buy goods and services from someone who sells them with a sense of certainty. It's not always easy to be confident in professional networking settings, especially when you're introverted by nature. However, you can boost your confidence by practicing as follows:

- Try to always maintain eye contact with the person you're conversing with.

- Use a friendly tone.

- Prepare a speech in advance and practice it. For example, if you're going to converse with a recruiter, do your research about their company (their policy, mission statement, and vision) and ask them follow-up questions.

Positivity

Positivity is almost similar to confidence, but it's more than just a character trait. Rather, it's a mindset and attitude that will keep you going even when the odds seem to be against you. If you remember how to have a growth mindset, you will also remember how beneficial it is to your career and how positivity is right at the core of it. Suppose you attend a networking event with the goal of making professional contacts that will help you further your career, but things don't go well. In fact, you're met with resistance or nonchalance by the people you'd hope to connect with. Would you give up on trying to make connections or keep it moving? A positive mindset will help you to keep trying and recognize that a bad day isn't necessarily a bad life and that if you keep trying, you'll eventually achieve your goal. Moreover, people are more drawn to positivity and optimism than they are to negativity.

Emotional Intelligence

When you are emotionally intelligent, you can understand not only your emotions but those of others. This is crucial for networking because oftentimes, the success of networking lies in perfect timing. Imagine approaching a recruiter when they are agitated or not in the greatest mood. You might be able to break through to them at that moment compared to if you had approached them when they were more relaxed and in a good headspace. Emotional intelligence will enable you to read non-verbal cues from the other side of the room to know who to approach, how, and when.

Friendliness

Friendliness is necessary for any setting and is characterized by simple gestures like introducing yourself, smiling, offering help when needed, and being kind overall. Friendliness will help you connect with people as they're likely to put their guard down around you and be less reactive. However, just like anything else in life, you shouldn't overdo it as it may come off as staged, suspicious, and sometimes even annoying.

Public Speaking

It's easy to think of being on a stage in front of hundreds of people when public speaking comes to mind, but sometimes it's just as simple as the spotlight being on you while you network with a group of people. When suddenly everyone is paying attention to you, and you're the only one speaking, do you get anxious when you notice or keep going with confidence and take that opportunity to adequately sell yourself? Public speaking skills will certainly come to your rescue and help you shine. You can practice your public speaking skills when you talk to a group of friends at a less formal event by minding your posture, tone of voice, pace, and how you articulate your words. That way, you will be able to shine when the need arises.

How to Improve Your Networking Skills

If you're worried that you might not have what it takes to network successfully, here are some tips to boost your confidence as well as skills for your next networking event.

Dress Accordingly

First impressions matter and dressing for the occasion is a must. If you want people to take you seriously and treat you with respect, you should dress professionally. Choose an outfit that says you're intelligent, trustworthy, and smart.

Take Note of Your Body Language

Keep your back straight and maintain eye contact. Also, don't forget to smile. Body language is important, and it's a good way to show the person you're talking to that you pay attention and that the conversation matters. If you're constantly on your phone or looking around the room, you might end up demotivating the next person and sending the message that you just don't care.

Ask Questions

Keeping a conversation interesting and engaging can be challenging, but if you ask open-ended questions like why and how, you will keep the next person engaged. Remember, people like to be given the opportunity to talk and to know that you're listening.

Think of the Outcome

You should have an end goal in mind. Why do you want to network, and what are you hoping to get out of it? This will help you to prepare, ask the right questions, and approach the right people.

Prepare Your Resume

If your goal in networking is finding career opportunities, then it's best to keep your resume updated. You never know when it might be needed. Recruiters appreciate people who stay prepared because it shows how organized they are, which is a requisite for most jobs.

Take Initiative

Indeed, good things come to those who wait, but in the business world, taking the initiative and being a go-getter will get you noticed. If people don't approach you, don't hesitate to go over to them, introduce yourself, and strike up a conversation.

Follow Up

Networking isn't a one-day event but a quest to create and maintain a relationship or bond with those you consider worthy. After you network, make an effort to keep in touch via email or text so that you're not forgotten.

How to Network When You Work Remotely

With the COVID-19 pandemic, remote and hybrid working became the order of the day, with 56% of the United States workforce working remotely (Boyarsky, 2020). While there are downsides to everything, remote working brings several benefits to employees and leaders alike, like no commuting hassles, work/life balance, and increased productivity. Some of the downsides of remote working include how one can find it difficult to "switch off" and risk becoming a workaholic, thereby risking burnout and how difficult it can be to network. Note that I used the word difficult, but not impossible. Moreover, a Buffer survey reported that 21% of respondents admitted to experiencing loneliness as a result of remote working (Boyarsky, 2020). Although people still hold Zoom meetings and FaceTime sessions, human beings, by nature, can't help but crave personal connections. However, networking can reduce these feelings of loneliness and create or build connections while increasing collaboration. If you've been struggling with networking as a remote worker, here's how you can remedy that problem:

Be a Part of LinkedIn Groups

LinkedIn is a great platform for job hunting, but it also offers an opportunity to join groups by location, profession, passion, and personal interest. Connecting to people with similar goals and interests is not only a great motivator, but you can also learn new ways of doing things effectively or stumble upon doors that will help you propel your career forward.

Use Reddit

Reddit is a great platform for connecting, with 330 monthly active users and about 138,000 active communities (Boyarsky, 2020). This platform has a group for everyone and offers instant communities for remote workers. You don't have to feel isolated and alone, and you can also ask for advice, explore your interests, and learn new things while connecting with people worldwide.

Use Slack or Teams

Slack or Teams are great tools for remote workers as they allow you to connect with coworkers from all over the world. You can even make lasting connections and friends with those with similar interests or who reside close to you. Everyone gets an opportunity to ask questions and contribute their opinions which is a great way to give everyone a sense of autonomy. For companies with more relaxed cultures, there are even groups to just relax and joke around on Slack. Remember how humor brings people together and creates trust? You can definitely bid loneliness goodbye if you actively participate in these groups, not to mention that you can learn something new every day.

Observe a Hybrid Routine

You can always go to the office when it's safe (if it's possible). Some companies have a hybrid policy where remote workers can go to the office once or twice a week to connect face-to-face with others. Remote working can get very monotonous, especially for creative people who get their inspiration from seeing different scenes or having face-to-face conversations with others. Thus, hybrid working can give you the much-needed opportunity to meet new coworkers, network with others, and solidify bonds with coworkers.

Join Online Meetups

Meetups is a great tool that helps you connect with those who share similar interests with and within your local society. Besides discussing work, there are various categories in meetups helping you to socialize and stay connected. These include hiking, learning a new language, photography, cooking, and more. Besides connecting with those who already share similar interests, you can choose to diversify and learn new skills. Whatever you choose, you will not feel isolated again.

Be Connected With Your Alma Mater

There are plenty of people from the school, college, or university you once attended who share similar interests with you. Moreover, there are even more platforms you can use to connect with people close to you or far away, like Facebook, LinkedIn, Twitter, and more. Striking up a conversation is relatively easy because you already have a school or college in common. You can enjoy reminiscing about school days before forming meaningful personal or professional connections.

Pursue Your Hobbies

Another great way to curb the loneliness or isolation that comes with remote work is pursuing your hobbies. If you have always wanted to take a language, baking, or piano class, this might be the perfect time to do it. By joining virtual classes to pursue your hobbies, you put yourself in a great position to link and connect with those who share the same interests. You might be surprised by the kind of professional doors this may open for you. Lately, many people are learning to code virtually and adding it to the list of skills on their resumes.

Volunteer

Tools like VolunteerMatch are great for finding online volunteer opportunities. To get started, you can simply type in your location before right-clicking on the "Get Started" button. You can then proceed to filter your search results by the opportunities that tickle your fancy. Volunteering is not only rewarding, but it will help you to build connections.

Utilize Virtual Coworking Spaces

Coworking spaces are a good alternative to working from home, but in the event that they are unable to operate, virtual office solutions like Sococo and Pragli help you connect with others regardless of location. However, there are various coworking spaces you can consider when they are open to the public. An example is WeWork, which is big on social events such as lunch and learning and happy hours. You can also join Workbar, which offers opportunities for social gatherings as well as nice and cozy workspaces in Boston, or Regus, which gives meeting rooms in 475 different cities in the United States (Boyarsky, 2020).

Be a Part of Virtual Networking Events

With the COVID-19 pandemic and remote work, the digital world has taken over, and trade fairs and seminars have been revamped. Thousands of people can now attend online events hosted by SaaSTR. These online events equip remote workers with information about future trends as well as what is currently happening in the business world. This gives you a chance to network, and who knows, you might just end up discovering your hidden talents or meeting people that will positively impact your career in ways you never imagined.

How Leaders Create and Use Networks

Ibarra and Hunter (2007) talk about Henrik Balmer, a production manager and board member of a relatively new cosmetics firm. Henrik hardly had time to network, and it was last on his priority list. Between handling the strategic issues of the firm, leading his team through a fundamental upgrade of the production process, and generally being the production manager of an expanding firm, he could barely find time to network. Not to mention that he still had to be at home on time so he could spend some time with his family. Balmer described networking as "the unpleasant task of trading favors with strangers," and it was a luxury he couldn't afford. However, Balmer realized how much he was out of the loop in and outside the organization whenever a recent acquisition was introduced in a board meeting, and being a fairly new production manager, he needed to secure his position within the organization.

Balmer's case is not unique to him, and leaders struggle daily to balance their many responsibilities and networking. When you have so much responsibility, making time to create and maintain new relationships seems far-fetched and unimportant. However, that couldn't be further from the truth. Leaders need to network because that's one of the strongest ways to secure their positions and drive the organization forward. Harvard Business School report following a cohort of managers navigating the leadership transition. This inflection point in their careers challenged them to rethink their roles and themselves. This analysis found networking to be one of the most dreaded developmental challenges faced by leaders (Ibarra & Hunter, 2007).

It's understandable that leaders are not always in a position to grasp their new role and understand that the relational part of their jobs is just as important as their technical functions. Most leaders rise to their roles by excelling in the technical side, but part of the strategic function leadership calls for involves building and maintaining worthwhile relationships that are good for the business as a whole. This is in no way a diversion from their day-to-day jobs, neither is it a waste of time, but one of the fundamental aspects of a leadership position.

One may also think that networking for leaders only involves mixing with those in similar positions but networking with those you're leading also goes a long way. Remember, a big part of emotional intelligence is the ability to empathize, and what better way to portray empathy than to those who look up to you and follow your lead every day? If I had not taken time to network with Julie, I wouldn't have recognized her dire need for work-life balance. The end result for her would have been burnout, which would have negatively affected her productivity and, ultimately, that of the organization. Thus, while making connections with people in high positions is crucial, don't forget that charity begins at home. You'd be surprised at the kind of teamwork you'll foster and promote if you take the time to network with those you lead.

Moreover, there are three fundamental elements of networking vital to transitioning leaders. These are strategic, personal, and operational networking. While operational networking helps to manage current internal organizational duties, personal networking helps boost one's personal development, and lastly, strategy networking sets the direction for new business and helps plan for future stakeholders. According to Ibarra and Hunter (2007), although managers differ in their approach to personal and operational networking, they almost always underutilize strategic networking. Here's an in-depth description and analysis of the three elements of networking and how they can help new leaders realize their goals:

Leaders who believe in their networking skills are often time operating at a personal or operational level. However, effective leaders should also focus on networking for strategic reasons or purposes.

Operational Networking

It's crucial for leaders to build and maintain positive relationships with individuals who are part of their team and without whom their job would be difficult and sometimes impossible. While this involves subordinates and superiors, it's far-reaching as customers, suppliers, and distributors also play an important role and have the power to either block or support a project. These are all players a leader should network with and maintain a positive and mutually beneficial relationship with. Here, coordination, mutual respect, and trust are of utmost importance if players are to accomplish their immediate tasks and produce quality products or results. While this is easier said than done, it's pretty much straightforward: The tasks provide focus and a clear-cut criterion for membership in the network (you're either relevant to the job or not, there's no ambiguity or confusion).

According to Ibarra and Hunter (2007), while operational networking came more naturally to the leaders they studied, it was characterized by blind spots concerning people and groups the leaders relied on to keep things moving or make things happen. They report Alistair's case, an accounting manager working for an entrepreneurial firm along with several hundred employees. Alistair received a promotion to financial director and started sitting on the board. Not only was Alistair the youngest board member, but he was also the least experienced. Consequently, his immediate response to his new role was to reestablish his functional credentials. The founder of the company hinted that the company would go public, and Alistair acted upon that by reorganizing the accounting department so that their books would be able to withstand scrutiny. While he succeeded in reaffirming and upgrading his team's competencies, he was ignorant of the fact that only a minority of the board members only shared the founder's ambition. A year later, when the board discussed whether or not to make the company public, Alistair realized that he was better off using his time to sound out his co-directors than cleaning up the books.

One of the challenges that come with exclusively relying on operational networking is that it's usually focused on meeting assigned objectives and not on asking strategic questions. As if that's not enough, leaders do not have much of a say in who they network with as that is prescribed by the nature of their jobs and the organizational structure, unlike in personal and strategic networking. Consequently, relationships are mostly internal at this stage, and ties are largely determined by routine and short-term goals. Likewise, external relationships with customers, regulators, and board members are not only determined by demands at a higher level, but they are task-specific or related. This is not to say that an individual leader cannot deepen or develop these relationships at will nor decide who gets priority attention. One has to keep in mind that operational networking gets its power from the quality of the relationship between parties and the trust they build between them. However, this kind of networking hardly offers leaders any help beyond the task at hand, given its membership constraints.

The typical leader was more focused on maintaining the existing network than building new relationships to deal with unforeseen challenges in spite of the task at hand (Ibarra & Hunter, 2007). One should always keep in mind that a transition into a leadership role calls for a networking shift characterized by an external focus on future obstacles, goals, and unforeseen circumstances.

Personal Networking

According to Ibarra and Hunter (2007), leaders like Alistair realize the challenges associated with an excess focus on internal affairs and networks, they seek to build relationships with those who hold similar interests as them outside of their organization. However, networking is not always easy, and one may realize they lack the necessary skills to succeed. This is when they also awaken to their lack of knowledge of business domains beyond their own. They may, however, gain new perspectives and advance their careers if they leave their comfort zones to get involved in professional associations, clubs, alumni groups, and personal interest communities. At this point, they can be said to be networking on a personal level.

Many leaders whose behavior was studied or analyzed did not see the need to create time for personal networks when they could hardly find enough time to perform urgent tasks. However, although personal networking may feel like a waste of time that could otherwise have been channeled toward more pressing issues, it is relevant. This is because these seemingly casual contacts can sometimes provide relevant information or links to referrals or mentors. Despite one's current success or stability, no man is an island in business, and the input of others comes in handy more often than not. Ibarra and Hunter (2007) also give an example of a recently appointed factory director who was faced with a turn-around or close-down situation that paralyzed his staff. In response to this, he joined a business organization where he met a lawyer who helped him navigate his situation. This prompted him to form networks within his company headquarters in hopes of finding someone who had previously dealt with a similar predicament. He eventually found two mentors.

Personal networks are also a good foundation for personal development and strategic networks. They provide a platform to work on your limitations before you begin creating connections on a strategic example. Some people are introverts who get stage fright or find it difficult to voice their opinions within a large group of people, others stammer, and others just get really anxious when they deal with people they are not too familiar with. I can not emphasize this enough—networking isn't a walk in the park. At least at first and for new leaders. However, just like anything else, when you practice, you will eventually master the art. It helps to do background checks on the people you will be networking with so that you have lots of open-ended questions to ask them during conversations. You can also start small, which may look like accepting one invite weekly to social gatherings. Eventually, you will begin to feel a lot more comfortable and gain more confidence. The good thing about personal networks is that you can use them to discuss problems and seek insights from those who have been there and done that.

Unlike operational networks, which are strengthened by the quality of relationships between parties and their mutual trust in each other, personal networks are strengthened by their referral potential. They are also highly external and characterized by discretionary people with similar interests and goals. The six degrees of separation principle suggests that one's personal contacts are valuable to the degree they help them reach the far-off person with the relevant information one needs in as few connections as possible.

Moreover, leaders who struggle to network at the operational level may shift their focus to personal networking. This in itself is a big step as it allows them to make external connections that may facilitate the organization's strategic goals. This may also help them to understand themselves and their external environment better, which aids in decision-making, planning, and forecasting. However, one should remember that personal networking alone is not enough to propel them through their transition to leadership. Indeed, one may create new personal relationships that can awaken new interests or help them achieve new influence within a certain professional community, but these ties may not come in handy where organizational goals are concerned. Most leaders who experience this downside may end up feeling like they wasted their time and efforts in networking, but in reality, they may have lacked a holistic approach that included three aspects (operational, personal, and strategic). The bottom line is that while personal networks are crucial and play a vital role in one's transition to leadership, they may not be as useful if they can't be assimilated into organizational goals or channeled toward influencing organizational strategy.

Strategic Networking

One cannot run away from the strategic aspect of management once they transition to a leadership position. If businesses only concerned themselves with day-to-day operations, they would not be able to withstand internal and external challenges, let alone competition from their business rivalries and new entries. The strategic level of networking calls for both vertical and lateral networking with other managers (functional or business units). Although strategic networking can be challenging, especially for new leaders, they can practice it and take it one step at a time. The starting point is realizing its importance and acknowledging that operational and personal networks alone cannot equip you with the ability to excel in both your short and long-term goals. Ever heard the phrase failure to prepare is preparing to fail? Being ignorant of the relevance and necessity of strategic networking can be likened to a failure to prepare. When you find yourself transitioning from functional to business leadership, know that it's time to delve into broad strategic issues and figure out how your contribution to the business as an individual can fit into the bigger picture and make a difference. In a way, networking at this level involves building relationships and finding sources that give you the power to achieve both personal and organizational goals.

Moreover, what separates managers and leaders is the ability to not only think short term and concern oneself with internal issues but to build relationships that can aid one in forecasting, figuring out how to maneuver in the face of future perceived changes or challenges, and solidifying beneficial relationships for the organization both in the now and in the future. What is the political, economic, social, technological, ecological, and legal situation in the business's environment? Is it likely to change in the near future, and how can your organization withstand the change in a way that allows it to sustain its competitiveness? Have you built solid relationships for the business to stay afloat where others are sinking? One can simply not underestimate the power of networking to get the right information that may otherwise not be common knowledge at a particular time or access to resources that may push the organization forward. If COVID-19 taught the business world anything, it's that the only constant is change, and one can't be in a comfort zone if they want to be part of a winning team.

A leader encompasses the ability to figure out where to go as well as single out the individuals relevant to the mission. A leader also has to recruit relevant stakeholders, diagnose the political landscape, rope in sympathizers and allies, and broker conversations among parties that are not connected (Ibbara & Hunter, 2007). Clearly, business leadership is something most people aspire to, but are they ready for the responsibility it comes with? Although seemingly intimidating at first, it can be done. One just has to keep in mind that a leader who doesn't concern themselves with the future of the organization and devise plausible and practical strategies to keep it competitive might not be a successful one and that strategic networking is right at the center of this.

It takes tactic and leverage for a leader to be fruitful in their strategic networking. You have to know your place, who is relevant for what, and how they can fit into the bigger picture of your strategy to help you realize your leadership goal. It almost sounds like a game of chase: Using indirect influence to convince an individual within your network to get an individual outside of your reach or network to take a necessary or needed action. After all, what use is a strategic network if you're not able to get information, resources, and support from one network to achieve goals in another network? When you network this way, you don't just influence your environment—you shape it. You can move and hire subordinates, change suppliers, or restructure the board. You just need to ensure your actions favor the organization's long-term goals. You can't be stopped, overtaken by rivalries, or drowned by unforeseen challenges when you run a business this way.

There's no doubt that strategic networking can be challenging, especially for new leaders. It's time-consuming, and it takes tactics and sometimes even wisdom. While one makes an effort to network, their operational duties do not miraculously disappear; they pile up and wait for attention from the same person who is networking for the better good of the organization. But truly, nothing comes easy in life, and you just have to find a balance between strategic networking and performing your operational duties. One is not more important than the other, and when one suffers, it might affect your whole influence and performance as a business leader. The business world is so unpredictable that forsaking strategic networking for operational duties may see you with no one to help when you find your organization in a sticky situation that may have otherwise not been a big deal if you had outside support.

How to Network Strategically

Strategic networking is difficult compared to the other two. It takes effort and dedication because you have to prioritize it just like your other duties and be strategic with your approach. Here are some of the tips you can keep in mind for your efforts to be fruitful in this regard:

Network From the Outside In

It's not easy to randomly strike up a conversation with a senior executive; it just might not feel natural. This is even harder if you don't share a common task or interest. However, you can pursue your interests outside your work and use the information and knowledge you get from your external relationships to build internal ones. For example, something as unrelated to leadership as joining a tennis club may easily connect you to people who hold senior positions in their organizations that you would otherwise not have dared to converse with on a normal day. You can learn a lot from them and use that as a basis for forming relationships with people or similar positions within your own organization.

Shift Your Perspective

Everything starts in the mind. If you don't consider networking a crucial part of your job, chances are you won't make time for it. Moreover, some people even look at networking as a cheat code that allows you to move forward because of who you know and what you know. This couldn't be further from the truth. Try to move away from this kind of pride and recognize that networking is as much a part of your job as your operational duties. One way to keep on track is to get a role model. When you see someone you respect walking the road you dread and doing it both ethically and successfully, you will rid yourself of any doubts you might have and be encouraged to follow suit. You can learn a lot from just observing. One can even argue that personal assistants who have worked closely with business leaders but do not possess the requisite qualifications to be leaders can make better leaders than those who are qualified. This is because they observe and learn the ropes by working hand-in-hand with leaders. Imagine how unstoppable you would be with both the qualifications and the know-how. Thus, do not be hesitant to learn from the best.

Learn to Delegate

If you're a new leader, delegating can seem strange to you. Understandably, you want to do everything yourself to make sure everything goes well and that you are competent enough to keep your position. However, there's no harm in delegating; you can even look at it as a way to groom others for leadership. Regardless of how important networking is, internal matters and duties still have to be efficiently dealt with. While accomplishing a task is fulfilling and may offer you instant gratification, the rewards of networking may take longer to materialize. As a result, many leaders choose the relatively instant gratification that comes with performing their operational duties. Sadly, the less they practice the art of networking, the less polished or efficient they are at it (Ibarra & Hunter, 2007). Remember Henrik? Instead of networking with fellow board members, he preferred to concern himself with restructuring the finance department, making sure the staff was competent, and polishing up their book. As a result, he was always surprised when a new network was introduced during board meetings or when members discussed issues with his role that he wasn't necessarily aware of. This is what happens when you prioritize one aspect of your job at the expense of the other. Delegating may help you achieve the much-needed balance between networking and your operational duties.

Be Consistent

As mentioned, the benefits of networking are not instant, and for a while, it may even start to feel like you're wasting your time and efforts. Most beneficial things take consistency, and networking isn't an exception. Sadly, leaders may network for a while but get derailed by the first crisis that comes their way. Ibarra and Hunter (2007) give an example of Harris Roberts, an expert in regulatory affairs. Upon realizing the need to broaden his network to be promoted to business unit manager, he volunteered as a liaison for his business school cohort's alumni network. However, he found himself overwhelmed by the tedious and strenuous approval process of the new major drug only six months later. Consequently, he dropped all of his outside activities. Two years later, he was still a functional manager and hadn't realized his dream of being promoted to business unit manager. By dropping his outside activities, he distanced himself from worthy networks that would have otherwise equipped him with the perspective and information that would make him an attractive candidate for promotion.

Ask

Effective networking is not characterized by having a large contact database or knowing a lot of people in high places. It is a deliberate effort to stay in touch with people rather than waiting before you urgently need something from them. What good is networking if you don't pick up the phone and make sure you stay relevant to those who are relevant to you? It's important for you to utilize every opportunity to receive from and give to your networks so that you're not forgotten. Can you really call it a network if you don't use it? I should think not. However, when you connect two people that can benefit from each other in relevant areas, you prove that you have something meaningful to contribute. You have to keep it moving.

Chapter 7

Communication

It is the long history of humankind (and animal kind, too) that those who learned to collaborate and improvise most effectively have prevailed.
–Charles Darwin

Building effective and healthy communication habits at work is a must because it's how you avoid miscommunication, arguments, and ambiguity. It's also how you build trust and strong teams. Workplace communication goes beyond saying hello, grabbing a coffee with a colleague, or sending a message wishing them happy holidays. It's how you convey messages to do with the workplace, and there's an art to where and how you do it. When workplace communication is done right, the company can thrive in the face of challenges and confusing internal and external circumstances.

Workplace Communication Explained

In very simple terms, workplace communication is any communication you do at work, about work. You're involved in workplace communication if you communicate about individual or group tasks, convey feedback, and update leaders or colleagues about the status of your project. If your workplace lacks effective communication, then confusion and role ambiguity are likely prominent. When that happens, you can throw any dreams of successful collaboration out the window, which would be unfortunate for every employee and leader involved and the organization's bottom line. It's also easy to hurt the next person's feelings when you lack adequate communication skills. Leaders who constantly have to give feedback to their teams, however unfavorable, have to be careful of this and know how to do it constructively and in a way that doesn't take away their team's confidence or kill their morale.

Moreover, workplace communication takes different forms: group meetings, face-to-face, video conferencing, or writing. It's important to take a holistic approach to all forms of workplace communication and put in the work to communicate effectively at all times. Below are more examples of workplace communication:

- receiving information
- verbal and non−verbal communication
- 1:1 feedback
- team meetings
- cross-functional task collaboration
- project status/progress updates

What Qualifies as Good or Effective Communication?

While there are various forms of workplace communication, there are fundamental aspects that make it effective or good, regardless of the communication form you're using. Here's a look at some of them.

Be Clear

It can be very tempting to use complicated words and jargon, especially when you're conveying a message in writing. Let's face it; it can make you sound intelligent every now and again. However, the goal is to convey your message clearly, and simple terms usually do the trick. Therefore, whether you're giving feedback, writing an email, or sending a message on slack, try to be as clear as possible and go straight to the point. Remember to be professional, polite, and precise.

Be the Person Who Solves Problems or Conflicts

Always seek to solve conflict and not create it, however tempting it may be. Office gossip can be quite comforting, especially if the person in question causes lots of chaos around the workplace. However, ask yourself if this reflects well on you and your values. Make it a point to only communicate when you're encouraging a harmonious existence or effective collaboration of teams, and refrain from harming others or bringing them down with your words in their presence or otherwise.

Make Room for Two-Way Communication

Effective communication also entails active listening, regardless of your position in the organization. Even when you're giving feedback, it's good to give the next person a chance to speak or hear their point of view. When employees are given a chance to communicate, they feel a sense of autonomy, which boosts their morale. However, even when you're communicating with a colleague, always remember that effective communication is a two-way street.

Tips for Effective Workplace Communication

Workplace communication takes skill: You should know when, why, and how to do it. It has many benefits, which is why this section is dedicated to equipping you with the relevant know-how of effective workplace communication. Here are some of the benefits it brings to a workplace:

- improves productivity
- improves employee retention
- reduces conflict
- encourages teamwork
- boosts employee morale and engagement
- promotes a healthy workplace and culture

Clearly, any organization would benefit from the advantages listed above, and every employee should do their part. You can try the following tips to improve your communication skills and contribute towards making your workplace a better place (Martins, 2022):

Know Your Timing

Most companies have different tools for communication. It's important to know which one to use for a specific message and when to convey your message. You should also know when to communicate in real time or if it's okay to send an asynchronous message (this is communication that does not call for both parties to be present at the same time). When in confusion, don't hesitate to ask a more experienced leader which platform is appropriate for a particular message. That is also part of effective communication that will erase confusion and save time. Examples of communication platforms include Teams, Slack, Zoom, Outlook, Gmail, PowerPoint, and Asana. Every organization abides by different communication guidelines. Therefore, it's crucial to always follow them to ensure you're representing your organization well to customers and stakeholders and to always be in sync with other team members.

Prioritize Face-To-Face Communication

A lot can be lost in translation when communication is not done face-to-face. Therefore, it's crucial to take the time to convey messages face-to-face whenever you can, especially when you're giving negative feedback or conveying a difficult message.

Where you could otherwise have been misinterpreted, your tone of voice, body language, and facial expressions will provide clarity. When you're not in close proximity to the person you wish to communicate with, you can always resort to scheduling a video conference. It will also help you to understand feedback from the next person as you will be able to read their non-verbal cues and tone, which gives you a chance to adjust your communication methods so they can understand and accept it better.

Enhance Collaboration Skills

Collaboration is at the heart of successful teamwork, and without it, conflict and lack of productivity will become prominent. Teams should always be able to communicate honestly and openly if they are to be productive. However, this doesn't necessarily mean that there won't be conflicting views and interests among members, but effective communication will allow for peaceful and constructive ways to deal with these contrasting views and find common ground or reach a consensus. Collaboration and communication work hand in hand, and one simply cannot thrive without the other. Therefore, knowing how to exist within a team and work with others means conveying messages to them without offending them and creating enmity, and the reverse is true.

Mind Your Tone and Body Language

A big part of effective communication is how you convey your message. Are you crossing your arms, raising your eyebrows, and coming off as judgmental, condescending, or irritated? Or are you relaxed, smiling, and making eye contact? Sometimes we give off cues that have nothing to do with the message we're trying to communicate and risk being misunderstood. For example, you might look angry because of a personal issue, but when you maintain the same facial expression when you communicate at work, your colleague may misconstrue that as anger towards them, especially when your feedback is negative. Thus, it's important to always relax your mind and body and mind your tone of voice when you communicate. This will help you to motivate your staff rather than demotivate them.

Always Foster a Two-Way Communication

It's crucial to not only give ideas as part of a team but also to listen to other people's ideas and views and put them into consideration. People know when you pretend to listen to their ideas and proceed to throw them out the window and when you actually take time to listen to respect everyone's opinion. When people feel heard, they feel a sense of belonging, and as a result, they strive to do their best to ensure organizational goals are met. Likewise, people also know when you're listening to understand or listening to reply, and the latter can create resentment and a lack of commitment. Autonomy is a big deal in organizations, there's no denying that, and rather than being created at executive levels where people contribute to big decisions, it can start at team level. You'd be surprised at the amount of commitment that will be encouraged by the team members. Also, when you merely listen to reply, you might actually miss key information being shared that would otherwise improve processes and productivity. Remember to maintain eye contact, nod, and respond accordingly when you listen to the next person and try not to speak when they are speaking. You can always jot down your question or contribution if you're afraid you'll forget by the time they finish speaking.

Ensure You Speak to the Appropriate Person

Effective communication has a lot to do with conveying the correct message to the appropriate person. It also has a lot to do with the setting in which you choose to convey your message or create a dialogue. When you convey a message to the wrong person, poor communication takes place, and this should always be avoided. If there's ambiguity about who you're supposed to communicate with, try to identify crucial stakeholders and ask for help.

Communicate Facts

Diana Chapman, the co-founder of the Conscious Leadership Group, recommended the facts vs. stories technique. She views facts as things that have actually taken place (things that the team would easily agree on) and stories as one's own interpretation of a situation (Martins, 2022). Stories are easily formed in the workplace and can cause division. Therefore, it's best to confirm anything and ensure you're communicating facts at any point to avoid causing conflict. For example, a female colleague spending too much time in a male leader's office can be misinterpreted as an office affair, but the reality is that they could just be working on a mutual goal.

Don't Promise to Perform Tasks You're Not Able To

Sometimes, we're only as good as our word, which means we have to be consistent in delivering what we said we would. It's easier to say yes to every task and deadline thrown your way as it sometimes appears to be the quickest way to get recognition, but it can backfire if you're not able to keep your word. Choose to be known for keeping your word and accompanying every promise with action. This means that if you say you will submit an assignment before the end of the day, then do so, and if you feel that you need time, don't hesitate to communicate that clearly and give your reasons where necessary.

Don't Be Stingy With Relevant News

Nothing says you're dedicated to your team more than sharing relevant information. Not only do you build trust with others, but they will begin to view you as an informed and integral part of their team. You can consider this as taking the initiative to lead. Whether you come across information that might help a colleague or your entire team through podcasts, scrolling on social media, or reading news articles, don't hesitate to share.

According to Jiang (2019), transparency and open communication are probably the two most significant characteristics of an effective and successful work environment. It also states that large U.S. firms can lose up to $47 million in lost productivity annually as a direct result of an ineffective knowledge-sharing culture. I have personally witnessed individuals not sharing, hoarding, or playing dumb with relevant information because they saw it as a source of power over others. When I found out, I took immediate corrective action to resolve their actions.

Ask Open-Ended Questions

A good way to engage in effective workplace communication is by asking open-ended questions (why, where, what, how, and with whom). When you do this, you give the next person a platform to share their views and knowledge without hesitation. When you ask questions that only require yes or no responses, the conversation is not very engaging, and it might end before all parties involved realize its purpose. Don't forget to listen attentively and ask follow-up questions.

Communicate Before You're Overwhelmed

Regardless of how dedicated you are to your work, burnout happens to the best of us. It's not a representation of incompetence or anything to be shy about. If Julie had not opened up to me about her hectic work routine, she would have carried on and eventually faced burnout, which would have defeated the purpose of why she worked so hard and sacrificed so much of her time in the first place. Communicating is important, especially before you reach a stage where you are overwhelmed. Therefore, if a task is too complex for you, it's good to ask for help, and if a deadline is too close, don't hesitate to communicate this to your leader. Likewise, if you're facing internal or external conflict that hinders your work, be sure to reach out so that you can get the help you need and be in a position to continue performing your duties without being overwhelmed. Thus, if a task is too complex or ambiguous for you or if a deadline is too close, it's best to communicate this on time. Likewise, if you're facing external or internal issues that hinder your performance at work, let your leaders know and get the necessary help so you can be in a position to keep showing up and carrying out your duties effectively.

Create a Talk-to List

Being organized is part of effective workplace communication. Therefore, whether it's face-to-face, email, or any form of communication, try to organize all your questions or create an agenda. Imagine sending six different emails to a coworker in a single day with messages that you could otherwise have sent all at once. It would be frustrating and might even reflect on you in a negative light. People are busy and seldom have time to go back and forth at the same time. You can create a list of people you need to communicate with and outline the topics of discussion or concern beside their names. That way, you save time for every party involved and portray your professionalism.

How to Communicate Effectively as a Leader

As a leader, you will give lots of feedback and convey lots of directives and instructions. It's important that this is done clearly and precisely, or instructions may get lost in translation. As you represent executive managers to the employees, you may also find yourself having to convey messages to the executive board on behalf of your team. Whatever the case may be, you will be required to communicate frequently. This may be a challenge, especially when it comes to giving negative feedback or when your message is met with resistance, but the good news is that effective communication skills can save you a lot of trouble. Whether or not you regard yourself as someone capable of workplace communication, there's always room for improvement, and if you're interested in learning effective communication skills from scratch, then you're also in luck. Let's get right into it:

Show Empathy

Empathy is a requisite skill for those in leadership positions. Without it, you may not understand the next person and be in a position to communicate with them effectively. You will likely communicate with clients from all walks of life as well as employees holding different positions, and if you can't understand their point of view, you might not be able to get through to them. For example, empathy will help you to consider people's health conditions before assigning certain tasks to them. Similarly, you will be able to remember people's names, pay equal attention to them during meetings, and be curious about their personal lives and interests. Leaders with empathy are able to communicate in a way that allows them to build and maintain relationships and create strong and trusting teams.

People are going through all kinds of stress, and a good leader understands the importance of empathy in their feedback and the communication they carry out in the workplace (Brower, 2021). Needless to say, such employees need empathy, and your organization might be at an increased risk of lower productivity, absenteeism, and even turnover if already distressed individuals are not treated with empathy.

Listen

It's important to listen to your staff and teams as a leader. This is because people often share new perspectives, ideas, and methods, and the organization stands to benefit from their insights. Moreover, when people are given a voice, they not only feel motivated to show up each day and give the best version of themselves, but they tend to feel like an important part of the organization. Indeed, the key to effective communication and leadership is active listening, and failure to do so may result in unpleasant circumstances for the organization as a whole. Of interest to mention is Intermediair's 2019 readers survey which identified or discovered failure to listen as employees' most common grievance with their leaders (Vanderheyden, 2021). As a leader, how can you take into account your team's input, know which tasks they enjoy performing, and understand their different personalities if you don't actively listen to them?

Not every leader intends to be a bad listener, but leadership calls for quick decision-making and problem-solving in order to keep things moving. If one isn't careful, this necessary aspect of leadership may hinder their ability to listen when communicating with their teams. Instead of taking time to listen to the next person's story or perspective, they may be quick to offer solutions or help. Therefore, it's important to evaluate one's self and try to know when to offer quick solutions and when to listen. There's no need to feel bad if you haven't been the most active leader there is, as leadership positions come with lots of responsibilities that consume most of one's time, but if you're willing to improve, then that's the starting point. Here are some tips to improve your listening skills (Vanderheyden, 2021).

Slow Down

Your mind is likely always thinking of your responsibilities and those you wish to delegate, but it's okay to slow down and listen to what the other person has to say. Are they asking for an extension to their deadline, or do they need help with navigating a certain system? Whatever the case might be, always take time to listen as much as you speak so you can understand your staff better and lead accordingly.

Pay Attention

Seek to find what you can learn from the other person's non-verbal cues, like body posture and facial expressions, so that you better understand their message. To show that you're not just listening but paying attention, you can also nod from time to time and ask follow-up questions.

Reflect

Reflect on your conversation and see if you have any questions you would like to ask or any additional information to add. Reflection is a good way to put things into perspective and make sure you and the person you're conversing with are on the same page.

Ignore Your Preconceptions

Avoid forming an opinion while the other person is still speaking, as this will likely reflect in your facial expressions and responses. This may discourage one from continuing the conversation and leave them feeling patronized or inadequate. Remember that part of active listening is seeing the world through another person's eyes and trying to understand their emotions and perceptions.

Polish Your Writing Skills

Communication skills are among the top three skills for effective leadership, and one way to thrive in this area is by polishing your writing skills. You will spend lots of time explaining yourself and clarifying things if your grammar and vocabulary skills are not polished. As a leader, you will communicate for various crucial reasons like inspiring, managing, producing, and partnering. People may not have confidence in you if your emails are constantly full of grammatical errors and ambiguous messages. Moreover, remote working is on the rise, and face-to-face communication will not always be feasible, making it crucial to communicate clearly in written form. Here are some of the advantages of written communication:

- It can be sent or read more than once.
- It is long-lasting.
- It can serve as a reference or evidence of communication.
- It supports remote working.

Leaders write for various reasons, each serving a crucial purpose to the overall success of the organization. Here's some insight on why leaders should polish their writing skills:

Writing to Include: 71% of leaders reported feeling informed about the operations and daily activities of the company, and only 40% of remote workers reported the same (Lebacqz, 2019). In today's diverse world, writing should be inclusive rather than exclusive, and it should promote diverse opinions and schools of thought and appreciate or acknowledge different cultural backgrounds.

Writing to Inform: Leaders have a duty to keep their teams involved and in a timely manner. However, remote workers listed a lack of information from their leaders as the top obstacle or challenge to their levels of productivity (Lebacqz, 2019). Therefore, one simply cannot undermine the importance of written communication in the workplace. After all, the company's mission and vision statements are normally in written form, and as a leader who breaks down the vision and mission into daily tasks, you should be able to clearly define roles and tasks for your teams.

Writing to Motivate: You can either write in a way that provokes feelings of inadequacy or demotivation in your staff or write in a way that promotes engagement and diversity. Clearly, no leader intentionally chooses the former, but a lack of writing skills may lead to it. It's crucial for leaders to develop writing skills that promote a growth mindset (which we know promotes or predicts success). One needs to understand their audience and take note of their tone, purpose, and choice of words in order to motivate the reader. Remember to practice and read articles about effective writing so that you continue to grow. A fixed mindset assumes writing is better off left to those with a muse, while a growth mindset seeks to learn and advance. Which one will you be?

Writing to Innovate: Successful teams are constantly solving new problems and tackling new challenges. But if they lack support from their leaders, they may be reluctant or even too afraid to innovate. Therefore, it's crucial for leaders to promote innovation by setting a tone of trust and expectation in their written communication.

Learn a Different Language

Multilingual teams are now more common, and globalization and technological advancements have made it easy for companies to hire diverse teams of people from different parts of the world. Leading a multilingual team can be challenging, but learning a second or even third language can help you navigate and lead successfully. Learning a new language is no walk in the park, especially considering all the other responsibilities that come with a leadership role, but stepping outside of your comfort zone to do so will separate you from other leaders and help you coordinate your teams as well as communicate efficiently. Moreover, understanding one's language puts you in a position to better understand their culture, allowing you to connect with them on a deeper level. Let's take a look at more reasons why leaders can benefit from learning a new language:

Cognitive and Emotional Benefits

Learning a new language can enhance one's emotional and cognitive abilities in two ways:

Cultural Competence: This is when people learn new ways of doing things. You can consider learning a new language as a window into a different culture. The process will further allow you to learn about their cultural evolution and history, which will help you to understand your teams better.

Enhanced Tolerance: You are more likely to be at peace in unfamiliar situations if you know the language. In other words, it enhances your tolerance for ambiguity. As a result, you become more innovative, giving you the ability to thrive in the face of uncertainty. You're also less anxious when dealing with change, which gives you a competitive advantage as a leader because change is inevitable. In fact, it is the only constant.

Moreover, nothing speaks of acceptance and understanding than learning someone's language. It breeds mutual respect and adoration, and as a leader, your employee retention and productivity rate will be exceptional as a result of this seemingly complicated but highly beneficial step. It's a good thing technological advancements have made learning of any kind easily accessible with tools such as Google Classroom, Microsoft Education, and Apple Education. Some organizations go a step further to invest in Learning Management Systems (LMS), so their staff can learn in their own space using a space comfortable to them.

Chapter 8

Driving Your Own Success

Becoming isn't about arriving somewhere or achieving a certain aim. I see it instead as forward motion, a means of evolving, a way to reach continuously toward a better self. The journey doesn't end. –Michelle Obama

You've probably found yourself wondering what individuals who get promotions and raises handed to them easily know that everyone else doesn't. If so, you're not alone, and yes, they do know quite a bit. The good thing is I'm going to share their secrets with you in this chapter from my personal revelation and insights from The Muse Editors (2022):

They Are Constantly Considering the Skills Relevant for the Next Job

It's okay to perfect the skills required for your job description, but people who drive their own success constantly seek to develop their already existing skill set. This makes them more attractive for promotions, raises, and even new jobs altogether.

They Dress for Their Desired Job

You need to set goals for yourself to know where you want to be within the next few years and which position you would like to hold. Figuring this out will help you spot those already in those positions so you can imitate how they dress and how they hold conversations, take initiative, and do business.

They Contribute to Meetings

People who drive their own success make sure their presence is noticed in important work events, and what better way to do this than to speak up during meetings? Get out of your comfort zone and make a suggestion, support a coworker's viewpoint, or ask a relevant question. This will be easier if you take some time to intentionally plan for the meeting using the agenda.

They Take Charge

The workplace is constantly faced with challenges such as low employee morale or productivity, project roadblock, and sometimes external factors like the unforeseen COVID-19 pandemic. Are you going to shrug and wait for things to get better, or are you going to be the person that finds solutions and solves problems? The latter would definitely work in your favor both in the present and future.

They Work in Harmony With Everyone

Everyone seeks to be in the good books of leaders and those who hold influential positions within the organization, but people who stand out make an effort to work well with everyone, regardless of their position. Working well as part of a team is important, and one needs to view everyone in the organization as part of their team.

They Affiliate With the Higher-Ups

When your leaders know who you are, it puts you in a better position to get promoted. Therefore, use every chance you get, without getting in the way, to make yourself known to those in top positions.

They Learn to Communicate Effectively With Leaders

Learning how to talk is crucial if you dream of becoming a leader one day. Those who have attended executive-level meetings will tell you the communication is a bit different. Learn the art of it, and you will eventually find yourself fitting in. You will also stop panicking when you're in the elevator with the CEO.

They Are Constantly Searching for Leadership Opportunities

People who drive their own success don't have time to wait around for leadership positions to be handed to them; they create the opportunities or take charge where it's relevant. From volunteering to lead a project, mentoring a junior employee, or offering their time to train new interns, they always jump at any opportunity to lead.

They Are Not Too Concerned About Perfection

When you concern yourself with perfecting everything you do, you're more likely to be reluctant to learn new skills or try a new role. This is because you would have to start from scratch and risk experiencing failure. People who seek perfection are more likely to have a fixed mindset compared to a growth mindset, and just like in Adam's case, that seldom works in anyone's favor.

They Like Their Jobs

If I could emphasize anything at all to the younger generations, it's getting career guidance. Oftentimes, people go for the loud-sounding programs or the ones their families approve of. Most Indian students are said to go for medical or engineering degrees as influenced by their families. In fact, a study revealed that most Indian parents are focused on their children building successful careers as adults, with 51% confirming that as their ultimate goal. Mexican parents, however, ranked higher than Indian parents in this regard (52%). When Indian parents were asked to rate the three most significant goals they desired for their children to attain as adults, 51% chose successful careers, 49% went for happiness, 33% preferred their children to lead healthy lifestyles, 22% said they'd be happy if their children just earned enough to be comfortable, and only 17% admitted to their importance of fulfilling their children's potential (Raghavan, 2015).

However, it's important for one to choose careers they would enjoy because if this isn't the case, going to work each day will feel like a slap in the face.

As an adult who has already pursued a career in STEM, I urge you to research the company culture, mission, and vision before you decide to join them. This will have a lot of influence on whether or not you will enjoy your job.

They Pay Attention

Active listening is more powerful than you can imagine. In fact, most employees look out for this quality in their prospective employees and those they seek to promote. When you give people your undivided attention, you not only motivate them, but you send a message that you care about how they feel and what they think. As a leader, your teams will be more efficient and motivated when you pay close attention to individuals.

They're Punctual

Being punctual says you take your job seriously, and you might not know this, but leaders do notice this. Also, it gives you a chance to select a suitable seat during meetings and conferences.

They're Always Professional

Do you display a professional demeanor every day by being supportive of your team, responding to emails on time, dressing well, and refraining from office gossip? Take time to evaluate your behavior at work and tweak whatever needs tweaking; there's always room for correction. You can technically be the best at your job, but your behavior can prevent you from getting promoted.

They Are Results-Oriented

Instead of just focusing on their day-to-day activities and accomplishing tasks, driven people focus on results. They measure their previous work against their current to see if they have improved in any way, and if not, they take the necessary action. Instead of thinking of how great the meeting was, they seek to see if they made any worthy contributions that will contribute towards the company's bottom line.

They Avoid Comparisons

Ever heard the phrase "comparison is a thief of joy"? It is, indeed. When you expect a raise or promotion because someone else got it, you might be setting yourself up for disappointment. Rather, try to focus on your own accomplishments and how you can excel in your role.

They Always Listen to Feedback

Giving and receiving feedback is part of most jobs. Therefore, when you give feedback, do it in a constructive manner, and when you receive it, don't take it personally. Exceptional people know how to take feedback into account and act upon it to improve themselves.

They Are Problem Solvers

Employees who are easily noticed and promoted by leaders know how to solve problems. Rather than complaining or dropping hints in the suggestion box, it's more beneficial to draft a possible course of action to overcome current obstacles and pitch it to your leader. This is not only taking initiative, but it's a way to show that you care about the competitiveness of the organization.

They Don't Indulge in Workplace Gossip

Every workplace has identifiable problems, and as mentioned, it's better and overall proactive to seek solutions to problems rather than seeking an audience to point them out. Are you annoyed with your leader because of the way they spoke to you the previous day? Then why not point it out to them respectfully rather than go around discussing how much of a pain they are? Whatever the case, office gossip can only lead to more problems.

They Socialize

Even though there's sometimes not enough time during working hours to perform your duties and socialize, it's wise to squeeze in some time for happy hour. After all, you know what they say about all work and no play. While the key to getting promoted is working hard, taking time to socialize with your colleagues and leaders is just as crucial. People tend to give promotions and more responsibilities to those they trust, and what better way to earn someone's trust than conversing with them and giving them a chance to get to know you?

They Excel Under Pressure

Pressure is part of any job, and the sooner you get comfortable with it, the better. Seek to challenge yourself by going the extra mile and completing tasks before the deadline. This will take you out of your comfort zone, and should real workplace pressure arise, you will be in a relatively better position to thrive.

They Are Self-Aware

They know their strengths and weaknesses, and they don't pretend to have it all figured out. They are not afraid to ask for help in areas they struggle with, and likewise, they willingly offer help in areas they thrive in. Besides knowing where exactly they need to grow, people who drive their own success seek to understand their leaders' goals for the future of the organization so they can align themselves with it.

Driving Your Own Success: Being Intentional

Maintain Work-Life Balance

You're at risk of burnout and stress if you overwork yourself. While it's commendable to go the extra mile for your job, there should be a balance. Also, you have to keep in mind that the quality of work you produce is more important than the pace at which you produce it. Most people find themselves so immersed in their jobs that even the activities they do outside work center around their jobs. For example, executives may meet to play golf as an opportunity to discuss business and find new business ventures. While this is effective, it means their minds are always saturated with business, and they never really get to relax. Such people are at a high risk of burnout. To avoid this, develop interests that have nothing to do with your job. For example, you can start a fitness journey, learn a new language, or attend social events. When you take time for recreation, you give your mind time to relax and reboot, which makes you much more productive at work.

Moreover, some people tend to carry their work with them wherever they go such that it's all they talk about, even at home, where they should be paying attention to their families. You should avoid this by keeping your personal life separate from work and ensuring that when you knock off, you do just that. Maintaining a work-life balance is especially challenging for remote workers as their workspace doubles as their home, making it difficult to clock off mentally and physically. However, you can overcome this challenge by structuring your work days as you would if you were working from the office, for example, having a strict eight-to-five schedule, Monday to Friday, or whatever works best for you. You can also have a dedicated workspace where no one interrupts you.

Manage Your Time

You can hardly succeed in your role if you can't manage your time. You will constantly find yourself lagging behind, overwhelmed, and unable to meet your deadlines. You can manage your time by preparing a schedule for the next day at the end of a current one or writing down your agenda for the day in the morning. Once you do this, you can sort your tasks by priority so that you do the urgent or most challenging tasks first when you're still energetic and do them easier or less urgent once after lunch when you're probably a bit tired and not in a good position to tackle challenging tasks. Likewise, when you're dealing with major projects, avoid feeling overwhelmed by breaking them down into manageable milestones and setting realistic deadlines for them. These time-management skills will have you easily meet your deadlines, especially when you minimize distractions and reward yourself after every successful milestone. Part of managing your time is saying no: Say no when coworkers need help with their tasks while you're still concentrating on yours or when you're bombarded with project after project while you still need time to complete the current one. Learn to politely speak up to your leaders and communicate why you need time before being assigned another project. Failure to say no will not do you any good, as you might still meet your deadline, but the quality of your work may be compromised.

Own It

Don't just own your successes; own your failures too. When you triumph, ask yourself what you did to get there and emulate it for future projects. Similarly, analyze your failures and seek to identify where you can succeed. Successful people are not afraid to admit when they need help, so don't be afraid to seek direction from those who have walked the same path, for example, leaders who once held the same position.

Six Reasons Why Drive Is the Key to Success

One can achieve just about anything when they have passion and consistency. Sure, you got a college education, and you're qualified for your job, but what will push you forward is drive. People who lack this element merely do just enough not to get let go, but those who are passionate about their jobs go the extra mile, and their final products are a testimony to this. Here's some insight on why and how drive will take you places in your career (Jobring, 2017).

Driven People Put the Business First

Although I encourage a work-life balance, there are times when everyone needs to go the extra mile for the business to survive. When these times come, it's easier for those who are passionate about their jobs to up their game and show up, even if it means going to work on the weekend or clocking in a little earlier than usual. This was one of the qualities that Adam lacked. He refused to flex for some weekend work where necessary, and as a result, he didn't realize the success he anticipated while others were getting promotions and recognition.

Driven People Radiate Happiness

Because they love what they do, driven people spread happiness in the workplace. Rather than complain and discourage, they motivate and inspire even without saying a word. Everyone wants to associate with a happy person; therefore, this puts one in a noticeable position, and people like this tend to be trusted with more responsibilities or leadership positions as they can be positive role models for their teams.

They Avoid Distractions

You can either spend time creating fancy PowerPoints or getting things done. There are things that are essential and things that are of little to no importance, and the secret to success is being able to differentiate between the two. Driven people ask themselves crucial questions like what their end goal is and what they will do to get there. By doing so, they are able to avoid distractions and concentrate on the tasks that really matter.

They Prioritize Their Health

Health is wealth, and one of the ways to ensure you give your job your all is to stay healthy. This means eating a healthy diet and sticking to a regular exercise routine. It can also mean refraining from intoxicating substances and getting at least eight hours of sleep every day. Not everyone needs to do heavy weight-lifting unless it's their preference, but making an effort to burn the energy in your body goes a long way, even if it's just taking a walk every day before or after work. You can also discuss with your medical doctor which exercise routine and diet is best for you if you have a chronic condition. Whatever works best for you, keep your body fit, healthy, and well-nourished. When you do this, creativity comes easily to you, not to mention that you will likely take limited to no sick leave throughout the year because your body will be functioning well, which translates to more productivity.

They Finish What They Start

Driven people always go the extra mile to finish what they start. Rather than procrastinating or doing things in part, they prefer to fully relax once they turn off their computers. This can be a blessing and a curse because sometimes it means rushing through things just to finish, and important details can be missed this way. However, when one masters how to set goals or targets and actually attain them in record time without missing any details, there's no stopping them.

They Command Respect

Driven people command respect in every room they walk into. People know how much they take their work seriously, and should they suggest something during a meeting, people will listen. When you're driven and have proved yourself over and over again, you earn respect. This puts you in a good position to lead.

Conclusion

Achieving success earlier in your career is possible, and I went to great lengths to explain how. From knowing how to communicate effectively, having a growth mindset, learning to view failures as opportunities, and driving your own success, there's no putting a limit to all the possible ways you can stand out in your career. Most people focus so much on perfecting their technical skills, but is this enough? When you go all out for your job: Work during weekends, clock in earlier than everyone else as well as clock out later than the rest, and neglect your personal life, you risk burning yourself out. I explained all the effects of burnout, including a loss of drive for one's work and an inability to perform one's duties. Overall, you go back to zero; isn't that ironic?

You can spend months working extra hard and neglecting yourself in order to gain recognition. You can even say yes to every deadline and every task thrown your way, but when you eventually burn out, you will lose motivation and thereby lose your ability to produce exceptional results on time. In the end, you might not gain the recognition you'd hoped to gain. It is for this reason that I strongly advise against overstretching one's self (unless the moment calls for it) and advocate for self-care, which is characterized by taking holidays, spending time with family, eating a healthy diet, regular exercise, and totally switching off from work to relax your body and mind. I advised Julie to do this after learning how she had been going above and beyond for her work but risking burnout. I can't emphasize this enough, work-life balance is important.

Moreover, if you learned anything, I hope it's the importance of having a growth mindset. A growth mindset seeks to evolve, learn, and move forward. It also recognizes that failure only means that you're trying something new. On the other hand, having a fixed mindset limits you, as it leads you to believe that people are good at what they do because they were born with the ability. This couldn't be further from the truth. I'm a firm believer in the fact that people can achieve anything if they put their minds to it. It's important that you keep learning. Avoid being like Adam, who was so comfortable in his role and routine that it never occurred to him that he needed to be a bit more flexible. Consequently, he felt frustrated when he didn't receive a promotion like some of his coworkers and couldn't understand why. The truth of the matter is that they were more noticeable because of their willingness to keep learning and evolving and to also go the extra mile for their jobs when there was a need to, even if it meant working during weekends every once in a while. Remember that the world is always evolving, and so should you.

I also talked about networking. Remember that no man is an island, and if you wish to move forward in your career, then take time to network both inside and outside your organization. Networking goes both ways; while the next person has a duty, so to speak, to point you toward relevant links, people, and opportunities, you have an obligation to do the same. Most transitioning leaders find it hard to balance their technical responsibilities with networking, and naturally, networking takes a back seat. However, networking is just as crucial as one's duties. It provides relevant links for you as an individual and the organization as a whole. The three aspects of networking outlined and described in the book shed sufficient light on this matter. Remember to follow up with any new individuals added to your network by staying in touch. Otherwise, what's the point?

It's crucial to also work on your emotional intelligence. It is one of the most relevant skills or characteristics of leadership. It involves being aware of your own feelings and those of others. No one admires a leader who shouts and screams when things don't go their way. Likewise, people appreciate leaders who are empathetic toward them. The good news is that no matter the level of your emotional intelligence, you can work on enhancing it. When you're emotionally intelligent, you're able to control your feelings, making it easier for you to handle pressure and disappointment. It also puts you in a better position to give constructive feedback (which people in leadership positions do a lot). As part of a team, you need to be a positive role model whether or not you're in a leadership position, and people will naturally pay attention when you speak.

Success sometimes takes walking the walk and talking the talk. Therefore, start dressing, talking, and thinking for the position you aspire to possess. Start imitating people who have done it and continue to do it well, and it will eventually come naturally to you. While certifications will get you the job, it is your character and ability to work well with others that will get you the promotion or raise, more often than not.

Lastly, don't be afraid to drive your own success by managing your time, enhancing your qualifications, refraining from workplace gossip, maintaining a work-life balance, being punctual at all times, and more. When you receive feedback, take it into consideration without feeling like you're being attacked, and act on it. Don't let self-doubt get in the way; you can certainly succeed early in your career. I wrote this book as a go-to guide for every STEM professional. Read it, meditate on it, live it, and watch your career turn into everything you envisioned and more. It will take work, consistency, and discipline, but such is the case with all things worth pursuing.

"Help others discover success!

Share your review to mentor others"

"Dear Reader,
Thank you so much for taking the time to read my book. Your support and encouragement mean the world to me, and I am truly grateful. I hope that you enjoyed the book and found it to be a worthwhile read. Please leave a review to help others hone their skills. I am so appreciative of all that you have done to help make this book a success."

Jeffrey Harvey

https://www.amazon.com/review/create-review?&asin=B0BTB68KRZ

References

Bansal, V. (n.d.). *5 emotionally intelligent habits for handling frustration at work.* TechTello. https://www.techtello.com/frustration-at-work/

Berlucchi, G., & Buchtel, H. A. (2008). Neuronal plasticity: Historical roots and evolution of meaning. *Experimental Brain Research*, 192(3), 307–319. https://doi.org/10.1007/s00221-008-1611-6

Boddy, N. (2021, February 4). *How to network in the age of social distancing.* Financial Review. https://www.afr.com/work-and-careers/careers/how-to-network-in-the-age-of-social-distancing-20200519-p54uda

Boyarsky, K. (2020, July 21). *10 ways to network when you work remotely.* Owl Labs. https://resources.owllabs.com/blog/remote-networking

Bradberry, T. (n.d.). *Emotional intelligence 2.0 step by step.* TalentSmartEQ. https://www.talentsmarteq.com/articles/emotional-intelligence-2-0-step-by-step/

Brower, T. (2021, September 19). *Empathy is the most important leadership skill according to research*. Forbes. https://www.forbes.com/sites/tracybrower/2021/09/19/empathy-is-the-most-important-leadership-skill-according-to-research/?sh=61c1ae813dc5

Buddha quotes. (n.d.). Brainy Quote. https://www.brainyquote.com/quotes/buddha_121206#:~:text=Buddha%20Quotes%20It%20is%20better%20to%20conquer%20yourself,by%20angels%20or%20by%20demons%2C%20heaven%20or%20hell.

Callahan, C., & Callahan, C. (2022, July 27). *Why employees should take a lunch break to boost productivity*. WorkLife. https://www.worklife.news/culture/lunch-breaks/

Casciaro, T., Gino, F., & Kouchaki, M. (2016, May). *Learn to love networking*. Harvard Business Review. https://hbr.org/2016/05/learn-to-love-networking

Cherry, K. (2018). *Overview of emotional intelligence: History and mea-

sures of emotional intelligence. Strategically Yours. https://www.strategically.com.au/pdfs/Overview-of-Emotional-Intelligence.pdf

Cherry, K. (2022, October 11). *What is operant conditioning theory?* Verywell Mind. https://www.verywellmind.com/operant-conditioning-a2-2794863

Christensen, L., Gittleson, J., & Smith, M. (2020, August 7). *The most fundamental skill: Intentional learning and the career advantage.* McKinsey. https://www.mckinsey.com/featured-insights/future-of-work/the-most-fundamental-skill-intentional-learning-and-the-career-advantage

Clifton, J. (2017, June 13). *The World's Broken Workplace.* Gallup. https://news.gallup.com/opinion/chairman/212045/world-broken-workplace.aspx

Craig, H. (2019, January 30). *The theories of emotional intelligence explained.* PositivePsychology.com. https://positivepsychology.com/emotional-intelligence-theories/

Davey, B. (2021, July 9). *Using the SCARF model to become a better leader.* Neurofied. https://neurofied.com/using-the-scarf-model-to-become-a-better-leader/

Davis, L. (2019). *The need for emotional intelligence in the workplace.* Grand Valley State University. https://scholarworks.gvsu.edu/cgi/viewcontent.cgi?article=1009&context=lib_seniorprojects

Enboarder. (2022, October 11). *Enboarder research reveals the value of human connection in the workplace.* Cision. https://www.prnewswire.com/news-releases/enboarder-research-reveals-the-value-of-human-connection-in-the-workplace-301645170.html

Express Employment Professionals. (2021, July 28). *New survey: Looking for a job? Employers value soft skills more than ever before.* GlobeNewswire. https://www.globenewswire.com/news-release/2021/07/28/2270394/0/en/New-Survey-Looking-For-a-Job-Employers-Value-Soft-Skills-More-than-Ever-Before.html

Farber, M. (2022, August 10). *Cybercrime damages to cost the world $7 trillion USD in 2022.* EIN Presswire. https://www.einnews.com/pr_news/585389499/cybercrime-damages-to-cost-the-world-7-trillion-usd-in-2022#:~:text=SAUSALITO%2C%20CALIF.%2C%20USA%2C

Ferron, L. (2018, August 13). *The 3 elements of burnout—They might surprise you*. Vital Work-Life. https://insights.vitalworklife.com/blog/2018/08/13/elements-of-burnout

Fischman, L. A. [mymollydoll]. (2021, June 30). *Overcoming frustration...* Self Improvement Blog. https://lesliefischman.com/2020/01/01/overcoming-frustration/

Gilar-Corbi, R., Pozo-Rico, T., Sánchez, B., & Castejón, J. (2019). Can emotional intelligence be improved? A randomized experimental study of a business-oriented EI training program for senior managers. *PLOS ONE*, 14(10). https://doi.org/10.1371/journal.pone.0224254ttps://www.goodreads.com/work/quotes/2766138-nonviolent-communication-a-language-of-life---life-changing-tools-for-h

Greedy, E. (2020, January 22). *Conflict a common occurrence at work*. HR Magazine. https://www.hrmagazine.co.uk/content/news/conflict-a-common-occurrence-at-work

Gong, Z, Chen, Y, & Wang, Y. (2019). The influence of emotional intelligence on job burnout and job performance: Mediating effect of psychological capital. *Front. Psychol*, (10). https://doi.org/10.3389/fpsyg.2019.02707

GoodReads. (n.d.). *Quotable quote*. https://www.goodreads.com/quotes/15158-i-was-never-afraid-of-failure-for-i-would-sooner

GoodReads. (n.d.). *Nonviolent Communication quotes*. https://www.goodreads.com/work/quotes/2766138-nonviolent-communication-a-language-of-life---life-changing-tools-for-h

GoodReads. (n.d.). *Phyllis Weiss Haserot quotes*. https://www.goodreads.com/quotes/9542393-all-successful-networking-is-dependent-on-two-key-things-reciprocity

Harvard Professional Development. (2019, August 26). *How to improve your emotional intelligence*. https://professional.dce.harvard.edu/blog/how-to-improve-your-emotional-intelligence/

Hastings, R. (2021, December 2). *How and why to develop a growth mindset in the workplace*. Emeritus. https://emeritus.org/blog/growth-mindset-in-the-workplace/

Hopper, E. (2020, February 24). *Maslow's hierarchy of needs explained*. Thought-

Co. https://www.thoughtco.com/maslows-hierarchy-of-needs-4582571

How to become a better communicator as a manager. (n.d.). Kelly. https://www.kellyservices.ca/ca/business-services/business-resource-centre/managing-employees/how-to-become-a-better-communicator-as-a-manager/

Ibarra, H., & Hunter, M. L. (2007, January). *How leaders create and use networks.* Harvard Business Review. https://hbr.org/2007/01/how-leaders-create-and-use-networks

Jiang, Z. (2019, November 14). *Why withholding information at work won't give you an advantage.* Harvard Business Review. https://hbr.org/2019/11/why-withholding-information-at-work-wont-give-you-an-advantage

Jobring, J. (2017, June 28). *6 reasons drive is the key to success.* LinkedIn. https://www.linkedin.com/pulse/6-reasons-drive-key-success-jenny-jobring/

Jones, J. (2018, January 11). *How reading increases your emotional intelligence & brain function: The findings of recent scientific studies.* Open Culture. https://www.openculture.com/2018/01/how-readi

ng-increases-your-emotional-intelligence-brain-function.html

Jongen, R. (2022, September 15). *5 growth mindset examples that you can use in your job tomorrow.* RevelX. https://www.revelx.co/blog/growth-mindset-examples/

Kapur, R. (2018, March). *Emotional intelligence at the workplace.* ResearchGate. https://www.researchgate.net/publication/323725847_Emotional_Intelligence_at_the_Workplace

Kurtuy, A. (2023, January 4). *11+top networking skills you must have in 2023.* Novorésumé. https://novoresume.com/career-blog/networking-skills

Lebacqz, E. (2019, February 26). *Why effective writing skills should be part of any leadership development program.* LinkedIn. https://www.linkedin.com/pulse/why-effective-writing-skills-should-part-any-program-erin-lebacqz/

Louick, R. (2022, June 25). *Growth mindset vs. fixed mindset: Key differences and how to shift your child's mindset.* Big Life Journal. https://biglifejournal.com/blogs/blog/growth-mindset-vs-fixed-mindset-differences-and-how-to-shif t-your-childs-mindset#:~:text=According%20to%20Dweck%2C%20as%20many

MacKay, J. (2018, August 14). *How a growth mindset keeps you competitive in a changing workplace.* RescueTime. https://blog.rescuetime.com/growth-mindset-future-of-work/

Maguire, E. A., Woollett, K., & Spiers, H. J. (2006). London taxi drivers and bus drivers: A structural MRI and neuropsychological analysis. *Hippocampus*, 16(12), 1091–1101. https://doi.org/10.1002/hipo.20233

Mark Zuckerberg quotes. (n.d.). Brainy Quote. https://www.brainyquote.com/quotes/mark_zuckerberg_453450

Markovic, I. (n.d.). *7 statistics that highlight the value of continuous learning.* eduME. https://www.edume.com/blog/continuous-learning-in-the-workplace

Martins, J. (2022, November 16). *12 tips for effective communication in the workplace.* Asana. https://asana.com/resources/effective-communication-workplace

Maslach, C., & Leiter, M. P. (2016). *Understanding the burnout experience: Recent research and its implications for psychiatry*. World Psychiatry, 15(2), 103–111. https://onlinelibrary.wiley.com/doi/10.1002/wps.20311#:~:text=Burnout%20is%20a%20psychological%20syndrome%20emerging%20as%20a,a%20sense%20of%20ineffectiveness%20and%20lack%20of%20accomplishment.

May, E. (2022, December 5). *The statistics on emotional intelligence in the workplace.* Niagara Institute. https://www.niagarainstitute.com/blog/emotional-intelligence-statistics

McGarry, O. (2019, October 22). *What is the 70 20 10 model in learning and development?* ELearning Industry. https://elearningindustry.com/70-20-10-model-learning-and-development

Morgan, J. (2021, November 18). *5 components of emotional intelligence.* Jacob Morgan. https://thefutureorganization.com/5-components-of-emotional-intelligence/

O'Hearn, A. (2014, December 9). *The 5 best strategies for learning on the job*. Inc.Africa . https://incafrica.com/library/aaron-ohearn-the-five-best-strategies-for-learning-on-the-job

Radparvar, D. (n.d.). *Becoming.* Holstee. https://www.holstee.com/blogs/mindful-matter/becoming#:~:text=%E2%80%9CFor%20me%2C%20becoming%20isn

Raghavan, P. (2015, July 18). *Indian parents have very high expectations about their children's education and careers.* Times of India. https://timesofindia.indiatimes.com/blogs/minorityview/indian-parents-have-very-high-expectations-about-their-childrens-education-and-careers/

Ricklick, M. (2022, January 19). *Professional self care: Tips to lower career stress.* Augurian. https://augurian.com/blog/professional-self-care/

Schooley, S. (2022, November 30). *Career success depends on your willingness to learn.* Business News Daily. https://www.businessnewsdaily.com/9256-career-boost-learning.html

Scott, J. (2022, February 22). *What percentage of communication is nonverbal?* Presentationskills.me. https://www.presentationskills.me/percentage-of-communication-nonverbal/

Simmons, J. (n.d.). *How to be a better communicator in 5 steps.* Monster. https://www.monster.com/career-advice/article/communicate-better-at-work-0117

Smith, J. (2013, May 3). *10 reasons why humor is a key to success at work*. Forbes. https://www.forbes.com/sites/jacquelynsmith/2013/05/03/10-reasons-why-humor-is-a-key-to-success-at-work/

Sun Tzu quotes. (n.d.). Brainy Quotes. https://www.brainyquote.com/quotes/sun_tzu_385644

Tchume, T. (2014, July 30). *Strategic networking and effective leadership*. Stanford Social Innovation Review. https://ssir.org/articles/entry/strategic_networking_and_effective_leadership

The Muse Editors. (2022, December 31). *47 habits of highly successful employees*. The Muse. https://www.themuse.com/advice/47-habits-of-highly-successful-employees

Tong, G. C. (2022, June 13). *Stressed and burned out? Quitting your job may not help*. CNBC Make It. https://www.cnbc.com/2022/06/14/stressed-and-burned-out-quitting-your-job-may-not-help.html

Tracy, B. (n.d.). *12 tips to set you up for success at work*. Brian Tracy International. https://www.briantracy.com/blog/business-success/career-success/

Valcour, M. (2016, November). *Beating burnout.* Harvard Business Review. https://hbr.org/2016/11/beating-burnout

Vanderheyden, K. (2021, July 5). *The key to being a good manager is being a good listener.* People Management. https://www.peoplemanagement.co.uk/article/1746234/key-to-being-good-manager-being-good-listener

WebMD Editorial Contributors. (n.d.). *Signs of frustration*. WebMD. https://www.webmd.com/mental-health/signs-frustration

Wilczek, F. (2015, September 23). *Einstein's parable of Quantum Insanity.* Scientific American. https://www.scientificamerican.com/article/einstein-s-parable-of-quantum-insanity/#:~:text=%E2%80%9CInsanity%20is%20doing%20the%20same

Winley, R. (2015, October 8). *Entrepreneurs: 5 things we can learn from Elon Musk.* Forbes. https://www.forbes.com/sites/richwinley/2015/10/

08/entrepreneurs-5-things-we-can-learn-from-elon-musk/?sh=61c8771e4098

Wooll, M. (2021, July 26). *A growth mindset is a must-have—these 13 tips will grow yours.* BetterUp. https://www.betterup.com/blog/growth-mindset

Wright, G. (2021, October 29). *How to apply the Porter's 5 Forces model to your SME marketing plan.* Smart Insights. https://www.smartinsights.com/online-brand-strategy/brand-development/how-to-use-porters-5-forces-model/

Young, A. (2021, November 15). *Millions of workers have made a "critical" error in their job - but got away with it.* Mirror. https://www.mirror.co.uk/money/jobs/millions-make-critical-errors-workplace-25463130

Free Downloads

5 TIPS TO PREPARE FOR YOUR JOB INTERVIEW

"OPPORTUNITIES DON'T HAPPEN, YOU CREATE THEM."
— CHRIS GROSSER

STEM SHORTS: FAST-TRACK YOUR LEADERSHIP

MIND BLOWING METHODS ON LEADING, INSPIRING, AND SUCCESS WITH OTHERS

JEFFREY HARVEY P.E.

www.apollodg.us

Learn the fundamentals of leadership today!

FREE

STEM SECRETS